THE

Wine Lover's

HEALTHY WEIGHT LOSS PLAN

100 RECIPES THAT LET YOU ENJOY THE HEALTH BENEFITS OF YOUR FAVORITE WINE

DR. TEDD GOLDFINGER
and LYNN F. NICHOLSON

New York   Chicago   San Francisco   Lisbon   London   Madrid   Mexico City
Milan   New Delhi   San Juan   Seoul   Singapore   Sydney   Toronto

Library of Congress Cataloging-in-Publication Data

Goldfinger, Tedd M.
     The wine lover's healthy weight loss plan / Tedd M. Goldfinger with
Lynn F. Nicholson.
          p.   cm.
     Includes bibliographical references (p. 277) and index.
     ISBN 0-07-147363-7 (alk. paper)
     1. Weight loss.   2. Wine—Health aspects.   3. Reducing diets—
Recipes.   I. Nicholson, Lynn.   II. Title.

RM222.2G597   2006
613.2′5—dc22   2006022864

For my wife
Melissa Goldfinger

1 2 3 4 5 6 7 8 9 10 11 12 13 14 15 16 17 18 19   AGM/AGM   0 9 8 7 6

ISBN-13: 978-0-07-147363-7
ISBN-10:   0-07-147363-7

Interior design by Village Typographers, Inc.

This book is printed on acid-free paper.

CONTENTS

RECIPES

FOREWORD

What could be better for health than the combination of wine and a diet from the island of Crete?

A moderate daily intake of wine and a Mediterranean—or, more specifically, Cretan—diet has proved to be far more beneficial to health than most of the expensive drugs prescribed the world over.

Consumed with a glass of wine, wild greens growing in virtually the entire Mediterranean area contain the right proportion of alpha-linoleic acid, which is indispensable for maintaining proper cardiovascular function and good health in general.

The Wine Lover's Healthy Weight Loss Plan and scientific works by Dr. Tedd Goldfinger confirm the half century of research that I have conducted into this relationship. A couple of glasses of good wine and a delicious Mediterranean meal—what could be more pleasurable? Knowing that this is, at the same time, the best way to protect against heart disease and illness in general might seem too good to be true. However, that is precisely what this combination does. I sincerely hope that this book of my friend Tedd Goldfinger has the success it deserves and that you enjoy putting his advice into practice.

Cheers!

Professor Serge Charles Renaud
Bordeaux, France

INTRODUCTION

A Perspective on Food, Wine, and Weight Loss

Leave your drugs in the chemist's pot
if you can heal the patient with food.

HIPPOCRATES

Many of you have tried one or more of the countless diets that have come down the pike. I too have fallen victim to fad diets, trying to lose weight and correct a poor self-image. I have seen many of my family members, friends, and patients struggle with weight loss failures.

As a cardiologist, I advise almost all of my patients to lose weight, because weight loss is associated with a lower risk of cardiovascular disease.

Truthfully, I have not always been the best model for lean body mass. I have often carried excess weight and an all-too-present paunch as a personal example of the failure of popular diets and other eating fads. Not everyone can achieve movie star looks from a diet plan, but better health is certainly a goal attainable by everyone.

For years, I put my patients on diets recommended by the American Heart Association and other credentialed cardiovascular societies. Most cardiologists and medical specialists, myself included, are only novice nutritionists, and we depend on diet plans and recommendations by national heart and dietetic organizations. Certainly, many dieters achieve the short-term loss of a few pounds with low-fat diets like that endorsed by the American Heart Association. Weight loss can also be achieved with carbohydrate-restricted diets that are high in protein and fat. These diets have worked well for a few of my patients and allowed them to achieve weight loss. Perhaps more important than shedding pounds and improving appearance, however, is preventing disease, rapid aging, and premature death. This is where these popular diets have failed.

Managing heart and blood vessel disease keeps me busy day in and day out. Obesity contributes directly and indirectly to this disease. Obesity is associated with a higher risk of heart attack and premature death. It leads to hypertension (high blood pressure), high cholesterol levels, type 2 diabetes, and depression, all of which are independently associated with a greater incidence of heart and blood vessel disease. As it turns out, despite reasonable success in decreasing blood cholesterol levels, a low-fat diet falls miserably short in preventing heart and blood vessel disease, as well as in producing sustained weight loss. The science of that failure is now understood, and I will explain it.

When I first entered the practice of medicine in the early 1980s, the American dieter was in the throes of the low-fat craze. This has continued for a very long time—only recently have we realized the dangers of an excess of carbohydrates. Along with the significant lowering of the amount of fat in the American diet—supported by every medical group in the country—there has been an exponential increase in carbohydrate consumption. *Energy food,* or so we have been told.

Simply put, you cannot expect to lose weight by consuming large amounts of energy food without exercising and burning off that energy. Our modern lifestyle, with its twenty-first century conveniences, has become soft. Most of us get much less daily exercise than we need. To make matters worse, we are not eating enough fresh fruits and vegetables. This has led to significant nutritional deficits. Obesity is the noticeable result of poor diet and lifestyle, but heart disease has become the silent killer within.

Statistics are screaming at us to change our eating habits: The American diet of fast and unhealthy foods has created 127 million adults who are overweight, 60 million of whom are obese, and 9 million of whom are severely obese. And the numbers continue to rise. That's why cardiologists and internists are so busy—there is no end to the line of patients who come to the cardiology clinic suffering from premature heart disease and heart failure due to, in large part, to years of eating poorly.

Phil is a commercial airline pilot who travels through my city every three to four months, where he completes his medical checkups. Phil doesn't have heart disease so far, but he does have hypertension, high cholesterol levels, and diabetes, which has grounded him all too often. This triad of overlapping risk factors for premature heart disease is termed *the metabolic syndrome*. Like many other middle-aged men, Phil has a rapidly receding hairline and has carried before him a sizeable gut. Stressful travel schedules and frequent eating out have taken their toll.

With our help, Phil has modified his diet and exercises every day. His wife is a red wine enthusiast, and Phil often picks up a couple of bottles of Australian red wine while flying in Asia. When he's not flying, he enjoys a glass of wine with dinner.

Phil had previously operated under the misconception that wine would jeopardize control of his diabetes. On the contrary, he has learned that wine, in moderation, will protect his brain, heart, and kidneys, all of which are targets of his diabetes. Now that he is on The Wine Lover's Healthy Weight Loss Plan, Phil has lost weight, passes his flight physicals more easily, and is more confident of his health.

What to do? The Wine Lover's Healthy Weight Loss Plan pairs the expertise of a practicing clinical cardiologist and a successful chef to rearrange your plan for healthy and happy eating. The search for healthy food and a diet that protects against cardiovascular disease—the number-one killer in America—leads us across the Atlantic to the vineyards of France.

Years ago, I became interested in early studies that reported the incontrovertible benefit of drinking wine in preventing heart-related diseases. This concept has been put into practice for decades in the Mediterranean region of Europe, as well as in other non-Mediterranean areas. In 1992, the British medical journal *Lancet* reported how wine drinkers in southeastern France are protected from heart attack and death by the wines they consume. These are the very same people who have placed on the epicurean table such heavily fat-laden dishes as foie gras and duck confit. Where one would expect a higher incidence of cardiovascular disease from eating such high-fat foods, the incidence of heart and blood vessel diseases was much less. Thus, we have the French Paradox.

This model piqued my interest. I began an intellectual pursuit that led me to closely study my own patients who drank alcohol, including wine. Several years ago, I was invited to the pioneering vascular laboratory of Professor John Deanfield at the University of London/Great Ormond Street Hospital, where noninvasive techniques were developed to study the physiology and function of blood vessels at risk of atherosclerosis. This led to a successful collaboration in the study of wine and cardiac risk, along with the formation of an international group of similarly interested researchers, epidemiologists (population scientists), and clinicians.

I became a protégé of Professor Serge Renaud, the French researcher credited with the discovery of the French Paradox, as well as the discovery of the valuable benefit of Mediterranean foods to cardiovascular health. Ultimately, with the help of Lynn Nicholson, an accomplished chef who has spent the majority of her professional life cooking among the vineyards of the Willamette and Rogue valleys of Oregon, I can offer a simple, medically sound diet that works to promote better health and consistent weight management for the majority of those who try it.

The Atkins and South Beach diets have taught us a lot about weight loss. You cannot lose weight and maintain that loss on a diet that is, for the most part, rich in carbohydrates. However, carbohydrates are not all alike; they differ greatly in their contribution to weight gain and loss. Fats, historically considered bad for dieting and improving one's health, are also not created equal. Some specific fats, known as essential fatty acids, are not only integral to health, but also help a person lose weight and protect against heart disease.

With the simple addition of a glass or two of wine a day and the application of certain dietary behaviors taken from Professor Renaud's studies on the island of Crete, we can boast of a diet that achieves short- and long-term weight loss *and* improved cardiovascular health. The Mediterranean coastal areas, including Crete (one of the healthiest places on earth), provide the secret of a healthier and longer life. The fruits of the vineyards around the globe add a healthy complement to healthy foods. The book in your hands has been inspired by contributions from the kitchens of some of our most creative wine friends. For you, this can mean a happier and longer life that meets and exceeds your genetic potential.

Mark has been a colleague of mine for years and, only recently, has become a patient. He's skinny by anyone's definition, exercises vigorously every day, and eats a predominantly vegetarian diet devoid of fats. He enjoys wine and prefers the dry white Pinot Grigio of Trentino–Alto Adige, learned from his years of schooling in northern Italy.

Mark surprised everyone by suffering a heart attack at age 64; he required coronary artery bypass surgery. The failure of a prudent diet and lifestyle? No! Mark's grandfather, uncle, father, and brother all suffered heart attacks before their fiftieth birthdays. Mark beat his genetic potential—and likely would have suffered a similar fate much earlier in life without the prudence of a balanced healthy diet and the protective effect of wine in moderation.

Let us not underestimate—or forget—the sheer sybaritic pleasure of drinking a luscious glass of wine with a meal. I sincerely endorse a daily glass of wine for my patients with heart disease. They appreciate the enjoyment it brings to the meal and the protection it offers in concert with their medical treatment. If the Russian proverb is true—"Drink a glass of wine after your soup and you steal a ruble from your doctor"—I say, let them steal my rubles.

The Wine Lover's Healthy Weight Loss Plan blends healthy, balanced meals and snacks with their appropriate wines, not only for taste but also for the maximum health benefit. The Plan is *not* about counting calories, fats, or carbohydrates. It *is* about eating fresh, seasonal fruits, vegetables, lean meats, fish, poultry, and whole grains and cereals, while eliminating saturated fats and bad carbohydrates from your diet. Because The Plan corrects deficiencies in some of your body's most important minerals, nutrients, and energy sources immediately, you will feel better within days. You will have more energy, feel less bloated, correct abnormal bowel function, enjoy clearer thinking, improve sexual performance, and more. With The Plan, you can look forward to the following benefits:

- A life prolonged beyond your genetic potential
- Increased quality of life in your later years
- Weight loss and weight management

- Improved physical appearance and function as you age
- Improved psychological attitude
- Improved cognitive reasoning, with protection against Alzheimer's disease and other forms of dementia
- A decrease in tension and anxiety, as well as a reduction in the effects of stress
- A reduced risk of stroke
- A reduced risk of atherosclerosis
- A reduced risk of gallstones and kidney stones
- Protection against food poisoning and other gastric infections
- A reduced risk of stomach ulcers
- A reduced risk of blindness
- Protection against arthritis, as well as relief from the pains of rheumatoid arthritis
- A reduced risk of catching the common cold
- Improved skin quality
- A strengthened immune system
- Anti-inflammatory, antioxidant protection
- Improved friendship, intimacy, and passion

The Wine Lover's Healthy Weight Loss Plan is more about engaging a lifestyle change than a diet of programmed deprivation. This book encourages the dieter to participate actively in the celebration of healthy living with the enjoyment of good food and the benefits of drinking wine. We explain how to stop cutting calories and embrace a more natural and healthier way of living. We emphasize the tradition of gathering with family and friends around the dinner table and taking the time to savor delicious food and appreciate good wine and good company.

This book guides you through a basic education on nutrition and health, as well as wine science and wine culture. It includes easy-to-prepare gourmet recipes with wine pairings to help you make the right nutritional decisions day in and day out. At the same time, it encourages a lifestyle that embraces moderation, variety, and balance.

Disclaimer

One or two glasses of wine daily can be part of your safe and healthy weight loss program. Moderate wine consumption does not contribute to obesity and can allow you to enjoy both the health and gastronomic benefits of wine while still losing weight. Alcohol, particularly wine, has significant benefits that improve health when consumed in moderation and with responsibility.

For some people, alcohol, including wine, may be unsafe at any level of consumption. A person who has a chronic medical condition such as liver disease, stomach disease, or bleeding disorder should consult his or her physician before beginning a routine of regular wine consumption. A person with a problem involving alcohol or other drug addiction, with a significant family history of addiction, or with an addictive behavior disorder, should not consume alcohol, including wine.

Please consult your doctor before beginning alcohol consumption.

GOVERNMENT WARNING: (1) ACCORDING TO THE SURGEON GENERAL, WOMEN SHOULD NOT DRINK ALCOHOLIC BEVERAGES DURING PREGNANCY BECAUSE OF THE RISK OF BIRTH DEFECTS. (2) CONSUMPTION OF ALCOHOLIC BEVERAGES IMPAIRS YOUR ABILITY TO DRIVE A CAR OR OPERATE MACHINERY, AND MAY CAUSE HEALTH PROBLEMS.

A WEIGHT LOSS PLAN FOR WINE AND FOOD LOVERS

In vino veritas.
In wine there is truth.
LATIN PROVERB

A crisp coastal California sauvignon blanc matched with herb-stuffed chicken breast with roasted red pepper sauce. A fruity Willamette Valley Pinot Noir sipped with fresh poached wild salmon from the Columbia River. A hearty Napa Valley merlot paired with Asian spiced duck breast. These are examples of the wonderful wine and entree combinations that await you as a wine lover, a food lover, and—yes—a dieter.

Keeping trim and maintaining good health are important goals as we age. Achieving these goals, while still enjoying the pleasures of food and wine, has been fundamental to the Mediterranean way of life for ages. The discovery of healthy eating paired with the natural health benefits of wine is central to The Wine Lover's Healthy Weight Loss Plan. Wine enhances the flavors of food and makes mealtime more enjoyable. It also imparts a significant health benefit, especially when paired with tasty foods that help you lose weight. As you follow the easy guidelines in this book, you will enjoy wine with meals and still lose weight.

Many of us eat for the simple pleasure of it, rather than for the nutritional value in food. I'm no exception to this. Many of us enjoy a glass of wine with our meals but fear the risk of added calories. I *really* enjoy a glass or two of red wine with dinner.

There's No Such Thing as a Wine Gut

Two thirds of all Americans are obese, or at least overweight. There is rising concern about the cost of obesity to human life in the form of chronic disease, especially heart disease. The medical community has been paying closer attention to obesity. There is also increased awareness in our schools and homes—and for good reason. The U.S. Surgeon General has established a reduction in obesity as a national priority and has called for immediate action: "The nation must take action to assist Americans in balancing healthful eating with regular physical activity."

Does this mean that Americans must deny themselves savory foods and a glass of wine with dinner? Not necessarily. Studies, such as that of Eva Vadstrup and her colleagues published in the *International Journal of Obesity and Related Metabolic Disorders* in 2003, show that wine drinking is not associated with weight gain, and wine drinkers are in fact leaner than non-wine drinkers. Vadstrup and her Danish colleagues demonstrated that moderate to high consumption of beer and spirits was associated with development of a larger waist circumference, whereas moderate-to-high wine consumption had the opposite effect. Who ever heard of a wine gut? A glass or two of wine each day can be part of your successful weight loss and diet plan for improved health.

What Does Dieting Really Mean?

Middle age has burdened me, as it has many of my contemporaries, with the necessity of paying attention to what I eat and how I live. My self-image and my health and longevity depend on it. As a cardiologist, I not only have to counsel my patients on healthy living, I have to set an example. My family and I—and my patients—can enjoy the many benefits of moderate wine drinking with sensible, delicious meals and still expect to preserve good physical and emotional health and stay trim. Drinking wine in moderation and eating food prepared from good basic ingredients can forever change the concept of the word *diet*.

Dieting has evolved over the course of our lifetimes from harsh caloric restriction to low-fat, high-carbohydrate energy diets, and recently to low-carbohydrate, high-fat fad diets. These diet plans demand cumbersome record keeping and strict counting of calories, grams of fat, carbs, or points. When brain-twisting, compulsive counting, and record keeping ultimately lead to failure, the result can be demoralizing.

Calories and fat grams are not counted in The Plan—just common-sense, natural eating with an orientation toward foods that are tasty and filling and that can jump-start your metabolism to help you lose inches. With this book, we introduce you to a diet with a scientific backbone and an orientation to the *enjoyment* of food.

"Wine Promotes Health" Is Not an Oxymoron

Wine, taken in moderation, is healthy and can promote a longer life. I encourage you to explore in depth some of the medical studies quoted in this book and the additional references cited in the Recommended Reading section at the end of the book. Don't be frightened by the science. The scientific evidence is stunning. Consult with your personal physician; we are confident that he or she will affirm that wine with healthy food can contribute to better health.

Skeptical? *Can wine actually lead to better health?* The answer is a resounding yes. Moderate wine intake improves health in many ways, but none is more significant than its impact on heart disease and its salutary effects in heart disease patients. Heart disease is the number-one killer of adults in the world. Each year, more than one million Americans have heart attacks; about one third of these die. By age 60, one in five men and one in 17 women have cardiovascular disease. *For many heart attack victims, the first symptom is the last symptom.*

The Beginnings of Coronary Heart Disease

Heart disease can begin early in life, often in the teen years. Our blood vessels are vulnerable throughout life to fatty infiltration of the endothelium, its innermost lining. The endothelium is at constant risk because of many factors, not the least of which is a bad diet. High serum cholesterol levels, smoking, and high blood pressure are well-known coronary risk factors that facilitate plaque buildup in our arteries, a process known as atherosclerosis.

Atherosclerosis is a consequence of negative factors pounding on the endothelium and ultimately leading to illness and disease. Atherosclerotic plaque can become inflamed and even rupture and bleed, causing a heart attack or death. Victims may not experience any symptoms of disease, such as pain in the chest, chest heaviness, or shortness of breath—until the situation becomes dire. This process is discussed in more detail in the following two chapters.

The French Paradox

In 1992, Professor Serge Renaud, a colleague who contributed the Foreword of this book, first reported that the French have an unexpected lower risk of heart attack and cardiac death than one would predict by their diet, which is much higher in saturated fat than that in the other countries studied. With its rich sauces and extravagant pastries, the classic French cuisine would be expected to wreak havoc on the health of the arteries of the French, to say nothing of the *frites* that have been exported to the United States as French fries.

How could the French escape the harsh consequences of poor health, obesity, and heart disease that would be expected from such a diet? The same ill-balanced diet in our country and elsewhere has led to an epidemic of heart disease and obesity-related disorders. When carefully analyzed, the factor that almost exclusively influenced the French resistance to heart disease and remarkably reduced their risk of death—despite a blatantly high-cholesterol and high-fat diet—was *the regular consumption of red wine with meals.* This apparent anomaly is known as the French Paradox. Not surprisingly, a less well-known Swiss Paradox exists in Switzerland's southernmost region, Valais—a French-speaking, wine-producing area.

The Plan Is Simple, Interesting, and Exciting

With The Plan, there are simple rules and no complex calorie counting or record keeping. The only items to record are the names of your favorite

---

THE LYON DIET HEART STUDY

Serge Renaud's insight was further illustrated by another landmark study, the Lyon Diet Heart Study, published in 1993. Professor Renaud and his colleagues in eastern France studied the effects of a Mediterranean-style diet, including wine with meals. The diet excluded foods that did not conform to the traditional diet of the island of Crete, Renaud's model for a healthy Mediterranean diet. Renaud had studied the diet of Crete for some time and found it to be a rich, nutritive diet, providing large doses of an essential fatty acid, alpha-linoleic acid (ALA), which was later found to be a critical ingredient in the healthy Mediterranean cuisine.

In the Lyon Diet Heart Study, researchers replaced butter with canola margarine, which is high in ALA. They educated the trial participants on the eating habits of Crete, which include lots of vegetables and fruits, legumes and whole grains, fish, and limited meats. Wine with meals, as well as lots of spring water, was encouraged.

Lyon is not a Mediterranean city culturally, and the locals were unaccustomed to this type of diet plan. The experiment was implemented, using classic educational tools, with 605 men and women with heart disease and prior heart attacks. The diet was a success, producing a 76 percent reduction in fatal and nonfatal coronary heart disease at the end of 27 months. Owing to the satisfying components of the Mediterranean diet plan, the dropout rate was low.

The Lyon Diet Heart Study shows that diet alone is a potent independent intervention to reduce the risk of heart disease. Certainly, no pill or capsule from your local pharmacy could claim a reduction in the incidence of heart disease even close to the results of the Lyon Diet Heart Study.

---

wines and wine producers and the years of the great wine vintages that you enjoy.

Although you will be applying some of the same principles from other popular weight loss plans, such as reducing simple carbohydrates and decreasing the size of food portions, you will be adding beautiful wines to accompany meals. The Wine Lover's Healthy Weight Loss Plan will help you shed unwanted pounds and feel better about yourself by emphasizing foods that are inherently low in calories, tasty, filling, and rich in essential nutrients that many of us lack in our diets. You will probably consume more fat than in a standard American weight loss diet, without the risk of increasing your cholesterol or triglyceride levels.

Traditional balanced American diet plans suggest that no more than 30 percent of calories come from fats, but inhabitants of Mediterranean countries often consume 35 percent of their calories from fats. The difference is the *type* of fats consumed. The Plan teaches you how to read nutrition labels and how to avoid saturated (bad) fats and eat more polyunsaturated—or, even better, monounsaturated—fats.

The Plan teaches you how to shop for healthy foods and prepare them with better health in mind. The recipes emphasize how to add the fresh flavors of homegrown herbs to your dishes, making each meal enjoyable and special. Best of all, we complement your favorite meals with suggestions for wines that blend with the flavors of the meal for maximum enjoyment, while adding important health benefits for your body's vital organs.

Good Foods in Balance

The Wine Lover's Healthy Weight Loss Plan brings together the right balance of nutrition, with protein (from plant and meats), good fats (such as omega-3 monounsaturated fatty acids), and complex carbohydrates (from whole grains and cereals) that are nutritious and filling in satisfying portion sizes.

The Plan's fundamental principle is to consume foods that help facilitate weight loss and to avoid foods that build fat. This means limiting simple sugars and carbohydrates, such as processed sugar, high fructose corn syrup, and white flour—building blocks for unwanted fat. At the same time, you will be eating nutritious foods that naturally promote weight loss by burning calories as they're digested. These foods, such as vegetables and legumes, whole grains and cereals, are themselves low in calories and provide essential nutrients many of us are unknowingly deficient in.

You must resign yourself to realistic food portions. "Supersizing" and reckless eating habits must go. In general, if it looks like too much food, it is!

How Much Wine?

It is healthiest to drink wine with meals and on a regular routine. The key is to drink a little wine every day. The Plan suggests that you drink one or two five-ounce glasses of wine with your evening meal. Men can have two glasses, women one. (The reason for the gender difference is explained in Chapter Two.)

Binge drinking or any alcohol excess is detrimental to health and uncivilized. Keep in mind that it takes only a small amount of alcohol, such as that from wine consumed in moderation, to help prevent heart disease and other chronic disorders. The benefits from wine's key ingredients (alcohol and antioxidants) are short-term and not cumulative, so it is essential that wine be consumed regularly with healthy food choices. Periods of abstinence from wine, from days to weeks, may negate the benefit to our body's metabolism and physiology, which I describe later in the book.

That said, The Plan is a safe and natural way to lose weight steadily and easily. But even more important, it allows you to achieve your desired weight and your genetic potential for health—permanently.

Lifestyle Change Is Key . . .
But Our Plan Is More Fun Than Others

Educating yourself about your own eating habits and proper nutrition is the first step. In order to make your weight loss permanent, don't think of being on a diet—think of simply eating better. It's not just what you eat that matters, but how you eat as well.

Slow down and take the time to enjoy your new foods. Make mealtime more than a brief, fleeting moment in your day. Read about the Mediterranean lifestyle in Chapters Six and Seven.

A basic knowledge of nutrition and the value of the foods you eat is essential.

Calories are a measure of energy. Calories in food provide fuel for your body to spend as energy. Since it burns energy, physical exercise is an important part of any weight loss program. Make time, if you can, for half an hour or more of aerobic exercise each day . . . walking, swimming, calisthenics, or a similar activity. Or just take more steps each day. My colleague Dr. James Hill, director of the Center for Human Nutrition at the University of Colorado, recommends walking as an excellent way to achieve fitness when you are beginning a weight loss program. By walking an additional 2,000 steps each day, you can burn an additional 100 calories. Keep your body moving: Grab a pedometer and your athletic shoes, and add more steps to your day. Exercise allows you to expect greater results from your new weight loss plan.

Finally, you must be ready to make a *long-term* commitment to these lifestyle changes. For many people, certain foods have become an addiction, much the same as smoking. Cracking this addiction and freeing yourself from the craving for poor-quality foods and a soft lifestyle are difficult—there is no doubt about it. But with commitment, personal victory can be achieved and the weight will come off and stay off.

Take Flight with
The Wine Lover's Healthy Weight Loss Plan
First Flight: Get Ready

It is time to make room for a new and healthier lifestyle. Put a hold on buying new clothes and take stock of your kitchen and pantry. Clear the cupboard of low-quality packaged foods.

During this flight, you will discover the resources for fine wines and quality foods in your community. Take time to meet the knowledgeable people at wineshops and food stores in your neighborhood; they can provide good advice and helpful direction.

Make space near the kitchen window for an herb garden to seed and nurture in the weeks to come. Set aside a cool, dark space in your home for wine storage—anything from a temperature-controlled specialty refrigerator to cardboard cartons placed on their sides at the bottom of the hall closet. Get excited: The fun is about to begin.

Second Flight: Jump-Start The Plan

To get your weight loss program off to a quick start, the next two weeks present limited meal choices at breakfast and lunch. You will be surprised what you can eat for breakfast—and still lose weight. Carbohydrates, especially simple carbohydrates, are restricted. They are concentrated early in the day, such as at breakfast, so you burn them off in your daily activities and don't store them as fat. Don't skip breakfast and cheat yourself out of the day's most important meal. You will need breakfast to get your metabolism going and be successful with The Plan.

Lunch is green and full of nutrients. Some extras are allowed, but rejoice in as much salad and vegetables as you want at midday. Avoid low-fat salad dressings; fabulous rich vinaigrettes await your pleasure and can be simply prepared fresh in minutes.

Dinner is a satisfying blend of a savory main course, vegetables, and of course wine. Extraordinary evening meals are paired with a variety of complementary wine choices.

You will visit your local wineshop for three specific bottles of wine each week for the next two weeks. New habits will be created. Shopping for food and wine will be fun, as you continue on The Wine Lover's Healthy Weight Loss Plan.

Third Flight: You're on Your Way

You have already shed a few pounds and are beginning to feel the difference, physically and emotionally. You have developed new eating habits. You have found some favorite wines and have identified flavors and characters in wine that you like (or, perhaps, dislike). Conversation with your local wine merchant has become more dynamic. You are articulating the nuances of wine flavors you experience each evening, for example, "Explosive flavors and aromas of black cherry and blackberry jam, highlighted by toasty Asian spices, pepper, vanilla, a little violet and rose petal, dried plum, and black tea" (a description of Robert Biale Vineyards Black Chicken Zinfandel 2003).

Meals at this stage are more varied and your healthy eating habits are consistent: healthy foods, moderate portions, and a glass of wine. If you're thinking about experimenting with food and wine pairings, now is the time. Use the fundamentals we provide for meal preparation and choosing wines; the rest is up to your imagination and creativity. The recipes provided here will stimulate you to fashion a cooking style with flavorful meal creations based on the ingredients of the Mediterranean cuisine now in your kitchen.

In the following chapters, the science of healthy food and wine consumption is clearly presented. We introduce you to "winespeak," the lan-

GIORGIO'S TESTIMONIAL

I was born in Torino, Piedmont, Italy, on April 23, 1943, and now live in San Benedetto Belbo, Piedmont.

As an international steel trader, I started my career when I was 23 years old and stopped just a few years ago at the age of 56, when I chose early retirement. My business took me all over the world, visiting steel mills in remote countries, as well as customers in large and small cities. I ate all sorts of food in restaurants from China to Mexico, from North Korea to the Republic of Georgia.

The frenetic activity of my business also implied a lot of flight hours, sometimes as many as 55 hours per month, and many hours of lost sleep. On top of that, I must admit that I had been a heavy smoker for more than 20 years, and reached a maximum of 60 cigarettes a day. I was a trapped citizen of Marlboro Country.

A long family history of heart disease, plus all of the above, could only lead to a heart attack at the age of 40. About six months before my infarction, I stopped smoking and gained 8 kilos (18 pounds) in two months.

My cardiologist told me to lose weight, exercise, and drastically change my way of life. I followed his advice, because I did not want to leave a widow and two young girls alone in this world. Since I was not a drinker, he suggested adding to my new diet a glass of good red wine at every meal. He also said that sex is good exercise, but only with a regular partner. This last suggestion was already my lifestyle; extramarital affairs are apparently too stressful.

Since then, I have followed a healthy diet and exercise every day. Now I eat fresh and steamed vegetables, lots of bananas, oranges, and other fruits.

guage of the educated wine connoisseur. We demystify the art of pairing foods and wines, with rules that are meant to be followed as well as some that you are welcome to break. We present three steps, or Flights, for your successful weight loss plan and food and wine experience. For your health and enjoyment, we present 125 delectable, easy-to-prepare recipes. We invite you to complement these with our recommended wines or alternative wine choices.

Whether you're a dedicated enophile or a beginning wine enthusiast, The Wine Lover's Healthy Weight Loss Plan will help you shed pounds while you savor tasty dishes and delicious wines.

I have pasta for lunch, fish or meat for dinner. To be quite frank, I rarely eat meat, and when I do, it is veal, turkey, chicken, or rabbit, never beef. To make a long story short, I follow a Mediterranean-style diet such as The Wine Lover's Healthy Weight Loss Plan.

My wife and I now live in the country, an hour's drive from the city of Torino, in the beautiful green hills of the Langhe area: a little Napa Valley caught between the Alps and the Italian-French Riviera. There is local production of great red wines, like Barolo, Barbaresco, Dolcetto, and others. We enjoy hunting for organic food, biologically grown (organic) vegetables, meat, and red wines. We now have a bunch of trusted producers and do not mind traveling several miles from village to village to get what we want. It is part of the fun.

We have our own vegetable patch. Every summer we enjoy ripe, juicy tomatoes, crisp zucchini, string beans, and other delicacies. Everywhere we have pots with basil, parsley, coriander, rucola, and oregano.

No butter in our kitchen—only olive oil that we buy from friends who have organically grown olive trees on the hills near the French-Italian border and produce their own extra-virgin olive oil. In addition to that, the nearby farmers inundate us with fresh produce during the growing season.

We buy fresh bread every day from the local bakery, but eat a small amount, only 50 to 60 grams, per meal. We use low-fat, lactose-free milk and avoid cream and butter.

I must admit I have not given up eating chocolate—rigorously dark chocolate, minimum cocoa content 75 percent, with cocoa butter—no other vegetable butter. My favorite ones are made with cocoa imported
(continued)

from Guatemala, Ecuador, Cuba, and Ghana. Apparently dark chocolate is good for my health, if consumed with moderation. I have difficulty defining moderation, but I suspect moderation for me would be defined as extra doses by others.

From time to time I allow myself some dessert, but just the good ones. We have a killer pastry shop in the nearby village of Bossolasco, only four miles away, unfortunately. I do not miss meat, but do miss cheese and butter. I eat less but better, and I never feel hungry. I never have a stomachache.

Since I stopped smoking, I have developed an intense and delicate taste for food, and . . . I have considerably increased my sex life.

I must confess some other sins. In the summertime, I cannot say no to the wonderful ice cream locally produced. My favorite flavor is, of course, dark chocolate, but I also like fior di latte (literally, flowers of milk). To feel less guilty, my wife and I decide to skip lunch and enjoy a fatty, cool, smooth, large gelato. Sometimes we are accompanied by friends, who visit from all over the world.

Today I am a healthy 63-year-old man, just a couple of kilos overweight. Considering my height, my perfect weight should be about 77 kilos (169 pounds), but my actual weight is 79 kilos (174 pounds). In my worst days, I weighed 90 kilos (198 pounds).

My suggestions to you guys out there: Eat healthy Mediterranean food, moderately; drink a glass of good red wine at every meal; and possibly buy and cook your own food. Avoid bad restaurants and fried meals. Exercise as much as you can. Do not fool around. Here and there, allow yourself to eat what you like best.

Here are some summer recipes we like to prepare when we have guests, which is very often.

Good luck!

Pesto Sauce (for spaghetti for four people)

2 to 3 garlic cloves
    4 tablespoons of olive oil
    4 tablespoons of freshly grated real Parmesan cheese
    1 tablespoon of pine nuts
      Salt and pepper
      A bowl of sweet basil leaves, washed and dried

Process the garlic, olive oil, Parmesan, and pine nuts in a food processor; salt and pepper to taste.

Add the sauce to boiled and drained spaghetti. If the sauce is too dry, add a drop of low-fat milk or boiling water.

Serve immediately, with basil leaves as garnish, and buon appetito!

Risotto al Radicchio (Rice with Radicchio)

2 tablespoons olive oil
1 purple Tropea onion, sliced very thin
   Salt and pepper
2 cups Arborio rice
2 radicchio, sliced
½ cup white wine
6 cups vegetable broth
1 cup Parmesan cheese, freshly grated

Heat the olive oil in a large pan. Add the sliced onion and a bit of salt and pepper, and sauté until golden. Add the Arborio rice and sliced radicchio; stir. Sprinkle with white wine and stir. Add the vegetable broth, lower the flame, and cover.

Check after 20 minutes and stir. Add broth as necessary and cook until creamy. Salt and pepper to taste.

Serve, topping with Parmesan cheese.

Tomato Sauce with Baby Zucchini over Penne Pasta

6 large ripe tomatoes (such as steak tomatoes), peeled and sliced
1 tablespoon olive oil
2 garlic cloves, crushed
   Salt and pepper
2 baby zucchinis, grated
1 small white leek, sliced very thin
⅓ cup fresh chopped parsley
12 ounces dried penne pasta, boiled and drained
¼ cup black miniature olives (optional)
1 cup grated Parmesan cheese

In a large pan, combine the tomatoes, olive oil, garlic cloves, salt and pepper. Add the zucchinis and leek to the tomato mixture. Let simmer for 15 minutes.

Add the parsley and penne pasta; stir thoroughly. Add black olives, if using.

Serve with grated Parmesan cheese.

TWO

THE WINE-HEALTH CONNECTION: THE SCIENCE BEHIND THE PLAN

> Wine is the most healthful and hygienic of beverages.
>
> LOUIS PASTEUR, FRENCH BIOLOGIST

The French Paradox: A Lesson in Healthy Living

*I*n 1992, Professors Serge Renaud of Bordeaux, France, and R. Curtis Ellison of Boston, Massachusetts, appeared on the TV news program *60 Minutes*. This brief appearance changed the way in which Americans and much of modern society perceive wine drinking. Renaud is the author of one of the most provocative epidemiologic studies to be published in modern times. He presents the indisputable fact that French wine drinking habits permit the French to live longer and to avoid heart attacks, despite an exceptionally rich diet that would otherwise almost certainly result in heart and blood vessel disease.

Professor Ellison had been a seminal investigator for the Framingham Heart Study in the United States, a longitudinal study of a New England population that has spanned decades. The Framingham project reported the influences of lifestyle on the lifetime risk of heart disease and cardiac death. It was from this study that much of our knowledge of the risks of high blood pressure, diabetes, smoking, and high cholesterol to heart disease was gathered. Ellison, in fact, had reported that drinking alcohol in moderation was shown in the Framingham population to have a clear benefit in protecting the heart against disease. This information, however, was censored from the formal reports out of fear that alcohol consumption would increase, along with the well-known deleterious effects of alcoholism. Keeping American society in the dark for years on the healthy effects of alcohol, particularly red wine consumed in a responsible and moderate fashion, may have contributed to the epidemic of heart disease we have witnessed in recent times.

The Statistics of Heart Disease: The Number-One Killer Worldwide

Cardiovascular disease is the leading cause of death and disability in the United States and is responsible for 53 percent of all deaths in women and 46 percent in men. Cardiovascular disease is a contributing cause of 60 percent of all deaths. It claims as many lives each year as all cancers, infections, lung diseases, and accidents combined! Not only a disease of the industrialized world, cardiovascular disease is the foremost cause of death worldwide, responsible for 57 percent of deaths in developing countries; it is the second-leading cause of disability. Cardiovascular disease includes diseases of the heart and blood vessels, and it includes hypertension (high blood pressure), stroke, and heart attack.

How the Heart Works

To understand how wine can help the heart, let me first explain what a healthy heart does.

The heart is the center of the body's circulation, pumping blood through its muscular chambers to all vital organs. Pumping about 70 times each minute, the heart requires oxygen and nutrition provided by its three main coronary arteries, which are muscular conduits that transport nutrient and oxygen-rich blood to the heart.

Coronary heart disease, the most critical form of cardiovascular disease, is the buildup of cholesterol and plaque in the coronary arteries that feed and nourish the heart. Coronary heart disease affects 12 million people in the United States, of whom 1.1 million have heart attacks each year; one third of these die. For many people, coronary heart disease can be prevented. Prevention, however, must start early in life, since the development of *atherosclerosis* (the process of cholesterol and fat deposition in vulnerable blood vessels of the heart, as well as of the brain, kidneys, and other organs) begins as early as our teenage years, and perhaps even earlier. Fatty streaks, the earliest deposits of cholesterol and fat, have been found at autopsy in young people who died from noncardiac causes.

The Evolution of Heart Disease

Over time, fatty streaks grow by disturbing the endothelium, the essential protective lining of the critically important coronary arteries. The endothelium, which is only one cell layer thick, prevents cholesterol deposits in the artery's walls and supports the integrity of the blood vessel in many other ways. The endothelium produces several substances, the most critical of which is nitric oxide, which keeps the arteries dilated and open to their greatest potential and prevents spasm. The endothelium also produces substances to prevent blood clots from forming that could result in strokes, heart attacks, and acute coronary syndromes. The endothelium produces inhibitors of growth factors that can cause fibrous and muscular tissues to grow, leading to complex and dangerous atherosclerotic plaques.

A normal, healthy endothelium is essential to cardiovascular health. A sick endothelium, one whose protective mechanisms have been disturbed and made dysfunctional, is a harbinger of disease and cardiac death. Endothelial health can be maintained by lowering blood cholesterol levels, not smoking, regular exercise, a normal blood pressure, and—yes—moderate wine drinking. Endothelial dysfunction is a process inherent in the aging process and is seen in elderly persons who are otherwise healthy. This is why heart disease and stroke is considered a disease of older people. To gain the greatest potential for protection against cardiovascular disease, prevention must begin early in life, then continue into old age.

Since the *60 Minutes* report on the good fortune of French wine drinkers—who overindulge in a diet rich in saturated fats and who smoke too much, yet paradoxically have a lower than expected incidence of cardiovascular disease—the French Paradox has broadened our understanding of how and why alcohol, particularly red wine, is healthy, protects against heart disease, and leads to a longer life.

Wine as Ancient Medicine

Is the French Paradox a new phenomenon? Not at all!

Wine was an important element of medical therapies until the twentieth century. The health benefits of wine have been reported throughout history. Records from some of the world's earliest civilizations have shown evidence that fermentation, the process of converting sugars to alcohol, was used to preserve foods and make foods more nutritious.

Accounts from some of the earliest societies note that wine consumption in moderation "made one better nourished and less prone to sickness." The Bible mentions wine in a positive light 650 times. Ancient Judaic records report "wine to be at the head of all medicines" and claim that "where wine is lacking, drugs are necessary." Hippocrates, patriarch of the modern medical profession, illustrated the value of wine in ancient Greece, considering "wine to be vital to health." A sixteenth-century German physician, Paracelsus, wrote, "Whether wine is a nourishment, medicine, or poison, is a matter of dosage."

Thomas Jefferson, the great American statesman, was a well-known wine connoisseur; he wrote, "Wine of long habit has become indispensable to my health." America's third president considered the impact of wine and health on his young nation and opined, "I think it a great error to consider a heavy tax on wine as a tax on luxury. On the contrary, it is a tax on the health of our citizens." And William Heberden, in his classic description of angina pectoris (the pain in the chest experienced by persons with heart disease indicating a life-threatening circulatory abnormality), wrote, "Wine and spirituous liquors afford considerable relief."

Since then, our knowledge of wine and better health has grown tremendously. The hallmark of wine's benefit to human life is most noticeable in the J-shaped curve discussed below.

The J-Shaped Curve

One of the most consistent findings in population studies examining the risk of death and alcohol consumption is the J-shaped curve. With alcohol drinking plotted on the horizontal axis and death rate plotted on the vertical axis, nondrinkers start off with a slightly increased risk of death from all causes, indicated by the small hook at the bottom of the J (see the figure below). A small amount of drinking or moderate consumption brings one to the bottommost part of the J, with the lowest expected mortality, and heavy drinking causes a sharp rise in risk of death due to the well-known perils of alcoholism: liver failure, cancer, death by violence, and accidents.

The J-shaped curve is true for all forms of alcohol drinking, that is, for beer and distilled spirits as well as for wine. The benefit of wine, however, is significantly greater than that of other forms of alcohol. Credible studies, such as the recent publication of the Copenhagen City Heart Study by my colleague Dr. Morten Grønbæk and his Danish co-workers, have

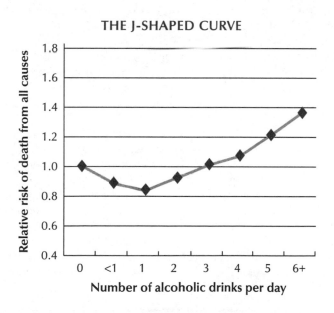

THE J-SHAPED CURVE

shown as much as a 40 percent reduction in all deaths with moderate wine drinking, and a much greater decrease in risk of death specifically from coronary heart disease.

In addition, a study by Dr. Eric Rimm and his associates, published in *Lancet* in 1991, showed that men who consumed two alcoholic drinks a day had a 55 percent smaller risk of cardiac death. In an earlier 1988 study, Dr. Meir Stampfer and his colleagues reported in the *New England Journal of Medicine* that, in a study of more than 87,000 women nurses, two alcoholic drinks a day resulted in a remarkable 60 percent decrease in the risk of heart attack or stroke and, in particular, a 70 percent reduced risk of ischemic stroke (stroke due to a blood clot in the arteries to the brain).

AFTER GEORGE'S HEART ATTACK

George has been a patient of mine for four years. He is 58 years old and has been seen at our clinic twice a year. He is tall and slim, and comes dressed in black jeans, a black shirt, black boots, and a broad black cowboy hat. He is the image of the Marlboro man, muscular and well tanned, owing to years of outdoor physical labor.

George had a heart attack four years ago, in large part due to excessive tobacco use, a diet full of saturated fat, and a strong family history of heart disease, to which he did not pay appropriate attention as a young man. As with many southwestern cowboys, George drank beer and whiskey to excess much of his adult life.

George survived his heart attack and set out to change his life. Today he eats a moderate, healthier diet, he has stopped smoking, and with his history of unhealthy binge drinking, George might have decided to give up drinking alcohol altogether. However, he now drinks two glasses of red wine each evening. We spend the first 10 minutes of his clinic visit discussing his physical activity and medications, and completing an examination of his heart. We then spend about five minutes talking wine. George prefers merlot and finds good prices at his local supermarket, where he has also acquired much of his wine knowledge. He is not happy with the disparaging portrait merlot is given in the recent motion picture *Sideways*.

For wine alone, compared to beer and distilled spirits, the J is deeper and broader, meaning that the benefit is much greater. Spirits, such as whiskey, rum, vodka, and gin, as well as beer, do reduce the risk of cardiovascular disease, because, as we will see, the alcohol fraction of the drink is responsible for a large part of the benefit.

These statistics and clinical findings make a convincing argument that a cardiac patient consider drinking wine. Take, for example, the case of George, the unlikely cowboy wine consumer, whose story is told in the accompanying sidebar.

Everything in Moderation—Wine Too!

Not only is wine the preferred alcoholic beverage for greater health benefits, it is also the only alcoholic drink that, when taken in moderation and with the prudent Mediterranean diet presented here, contributes to weight loss and a smaller waist.

Unlike beer and spirits, wine is *the beverage of moderation.* Moderate wine drinking and a Mediterranean diet are the key to better health and a longer life. Wine is meant to be consumed with food, at the table, over conversation, and with family and friends. Families should be encouraged to share in the wine and food experience at the dinner table, as has been done for centuries in Mediterranean Europe. Children should be exposed to responsible wine drinking early on, so that when they are of age, they will act responsibly and not partake in excessive alcohol drinking.

It is commonplace at the European table for children to participate in the wine experience. I have noticed this over several pleasurable visits with my friend Bernard and his family in Bordeaux. Bernard's young sons, Alexander and Pierre, are given a juice-sized glass of water with a generous splash of red wine at dinner. In this case, the wine was produced from the family's own vineyards, although it is sometimes supplied by friends or acquaintances in the village. Alex, the older of the two, fetches the evening's beverage from the cellar, and Pierre inspects the wine for color and clarity. The children experience early training of their palate for later wine appreciation. The process most sensitively instills in them the tradition of wine at the dinner table with family, friends, and guests. Everyone at the

RED WINE IN THE EVENING

Ned has had heart disease for more than 25 years. He is a war hero and survived Iwo Jima with a dozen bullet wounds during World War Two. Ned had coronary artery bypass surgery before I met him nearly 20 years ago. Since then, he has required several coronary angioplasties (balloon procedures that open narrowings in plaque-laden coronary arteries) and placement of coronary artery stents (stainless steel mesh tubes) in his compromised blood vessels and bypass conduits.

Ned is now 85 years old. He shows his age, with crippling arthritis and a deeply wrinkled brow that hardens his otherwise soft expression. His aging exterior forewarns of the risks he faces each day with his aging heart. Ned wasn't a drinker before we met, nor did he have any interest in wine. As a career military man, wine just didn't suit his lifestyle. With the support of his family over the past several years, however, Ned now takes four ounces of red wine in a glass of sparkling water each night, and he feels better doing it. He likes the flavor, more subtle when diluted, and it relaxes him. He sleeps better, and he's convinced it helps reduce his arthritis pain. He knows it helps protect his heart.

table enjoys the meal, and the wine complements the food brilliantly. The dinner conversation is lively, and no one leaves the table intoxicated. It would be an insult to the cook and the hosts if that were so.

The Biology of Wine

The health benefit of wine is derived in equal parts from the alcohol and the nonalcoholic components of wine. Alcohol is one of the most potent means of increasing high-density lipoprotein (HDL), the good cholesterol. HDL is good because it acts as a scavenger in removing cholesterol and fat from arterial walls and bringing them to the liver for degradation and elimination. This is often the hardest of the lipoproteins to optimize with medical therapy. Statins, popular drugs used to lower cholesterol levels, have little effect on HDL cholesterol. Diet and exercise increase HDL cholesterol, but not to the extent that moderate alcohol consumption can. Levels of low-density lipoprotein (LDL), the bad cholesterol, is unaffected by alcohol. However, LDL can be modified by the nonalcoholic components of wine to render it less harmful to the blood vessels and vascular system.

Alcohol has a potent effect in blocking platelet activity in the blood. Platelets are small cells that circulate in the bloodstream and initiate blood clots, when necessary, to repair cuts and bruises. Inflammation and disruption of arterial walls that occur as a result of minor trauma to the inside of blood vessels, such as may be caused by high cholesterol levels or high blood pressure, attract platelets as the body's natural response to injury. Platelets clump together and can snowball into blood clots that seriously obstruct blood flow. Alcohol is able to make platelets less likely or able to clump, a process called platelet inhibition. Similar to aspirin, alcohol protects against the harmful effects of blood clotting in the vascular system, which could result in heart attack or stroke.

Dr. Arthur Klatsky, a research cardiologist and noted alcohol specialist from the Kaiser Permanente Medical Center in Oakland, California, has reported that at least half of the benefits of wine are from the alcohol itself. In studying the enhanced survival of the French wine drinker, Professor Serge Renaud noted that the French did not seem to have higher HDL levels than other populations who drank far less wine. He believes that the greatest benefit is from wine's ability to inhibit platelets and reduce blood clots.

Wine Under the Microscope

Some of the more recent and provocative findings in the health benefits of wine have been in the effects of its nonalcoholic components. Wine contains many polyphenols, most derived from the grape's seeds and skin. Polyphenols are organic compounds that have a number of important functions in wine and contribute to its bitterness and astringency, especially in red wine. The color of red wine is caused by polyphenolic pigments. Polyphenols are also a key wine preservative and allow the graceful aging and maturation of flavor and color in wine. Wine polyphenols include specific flavonoid and nonflavonoid substances, such as hydroxycinnamates, hydroxybenzoates, stilbenes, flavonols, and anthocyanins.

The total amount of polyphenols in a glass of red wine is about 200 mg, compared to about 40 mg in a glass of white wine; there are five times more bioactive life-sustaining polyphenols in red wine than in white wine.

Antioxidants for Health and Longevity

Polyphenols have many important biological properties. They are powerful antioxidants, more so than popular vitamin supplements, such as vitamins C and E. Scientists are able to measure a considerable increase in the antioxidant capacity of the blood as early as 90 minutes after a glass of wine is consumed. Red wine increases the serum antioxidant capacity almost five times higher than white wine.

Why are antioxidants important? For cardiovascular disease, oxidation of LDL (the bad cholesterol) is a critical reaction that makes LDL more harmful. Oxidized LDL can more easily penetrate the endothelial barrier of blood vessels, incite inflammation, and attract other fats and abnormal cell components that make up atherosclerotic plaque. In the laboratory, adding wine polyphenols to human LDL reduces oxidation susceptibility by up to 98 percent. Oxidation reactions are thought to be responsible for various cancers and age-related illnesses.

The abundance of antioxidants in The Wine Lover's Healthy Weight Loss Plan is essential. Many fruits and vegetables in The Plan's recipes are high in antioxidants. Berries such as blackberries, blueberries, and raspberries are loaded with healthy antioxidants, just like red wine grapes. It is no wonder that through the ages wine drinkers not only have less heart disease, but also have fewer cancers and age more gracefully. Skin, bones, and organs seem to be more resistant to the usual signs of old age. Elderly wine drinkers also have a lower risk of developing dementia than non-drinkers.

Purple grape juice is *not* a perfect substitute for red wine. For persons who are unable to drink alcohol for medical or religious reasons, purple grape juice can offer a healthy supply of antioxidants, but an important ingredient, the alcohol, is missing, and the unfermented sugars in the juice add calories. Scientific studies that suggest purple grape juice is the equal of red wine in salutary effect are limited in number—and suspiciously sponsored by the grape juice industry. For non-alcohol drinkers, grape seed extract or other grape-derived supplements may be a reasonable addition to the diet without adding sugars and calories.

When one considers the cascade of events in the formation of cardiovascular disease, one cannot ignore the fact that wine and its components block almost every abnormal event that leads to the formation of heart and blood vessel disease. Heart disease also shares common pathologic events that lead to other diseases, and so wine's effect in maintaining good health is experienced everywhere in the human body.

Specifically, moderate red wine consumption reduces the level of C-reactive protein (CRP), an important biomarker indicating heart disease risk. Red wine inhibits blood vessel wall thickening, an abnormal process known as hyperplasia. It reduces the attachment of white blood cells (which breed inflammation) to the endothelium and inhibits the cellular molecules on the endothelial surface that bind inflammatory cells. Red wine reduces foamy, plaque-initiating cell changes in blood vessels and decreases the burden of clot-forming factors in blood vessels.

Resveratrol: An Important Wine Polyphenol

Resveratrol inhibits many of the molecular factors that cause inflammation and blocks the proliferation not only of the inflammatory factors, but also of the many other components that cause atherosclerosis.

Resveratrol is abundant in the grape but can also be found in various plants, berries, and peanuts. Convincing evidence indicates that resveratrol has beneficial effects in the brain and neurological system, in the liver and gastrointestinal system, and in the cardiovascular system. A most striking recent discovery of the biological activities of resveratrol has been its cancer-prevention potential. In fact, resveratrol has been demonstrated to block the process of carcinogenesis (cancer formation) at various stages, including tumor initiation, promotion, and progression. One of the most probable mechanisms for this benefit involves quieting the body's inflammatory response by inhibiting the production and release of inflammatory mediators and inhibiting activated immune cells.

Much attention has been paid recently to data showing resveratrol's effect in prolonging the lifespan of yeast and flies. The human organism is a great deal different from the yeast cell and housefly, yet resveratrol is being investigated as an antiaging agent in the treatment of many age-related human diseases.

Wine—A Living Beverage

Wine is a natural beverage; it contains no preservatives. Julia Child is credited with defining wine as a "living beverage." Wine has a life cycle that spans youth, maturity, old age, and death.

In general, the less the winemaker manipulates the process of wine-making, the better and more desirable is the final product. Filtering, often performed to achieve greater clarity in wine, removes many of the healthy antioxidants and nutrients that support better health. Many winemakers restrain from filtering the wine before bottling for this very reason. A cloudy glass of wine is not necessarily a bad glass of wine. Nor is the presence of sediment at the bottom of the glass a sign of poor quality. It is actually an indication that the winemaker respects the process that nature had intended for the grape. An Italian friend of mine observes the sediment at the bottom of the wineglass, murmurs a salutation to health, and stirs in a bit of water to emulsify the sediment so that he can swallow it in one gulp. Wine that is left to its natural tendencies supports and enhances life.

More Evidence of the Benefits of Wine

Growing up around Bordeaux,
you know instinctively that wine is good for you.
My grandparents, their friends, all lived to be eighty or ninety.
I knew there was some special reason.

PROFESSOR SERGE RENAUD,
FATHER OF THE FRENCH PARADOX

In a medical letter in 2003, Giuseppe Trapani reported that on the Mediterranean island of Pantelleria, where the islanders consume, on average, about 350 ml of locally produced red wine daily (about half of a standard bottle), there are far fewer intestinal disorders than in similar island communities. The incidence of chronic bacterial urinary infection is 30 percent lower than in other populations.

In a 2004 review of relevant studies by Luc Letenneur published by Université Victor Segalen Bordeaux II, an inverse relationship was shown between moderate wine drinking and the incidence of dementia and Alzheimer's disease. These results were confirmed by a study in Rotterdam, the Netherlands, where light to moderate drinking (one to three drinks per day) was shown to be associated with a 43 percent lower risk of any dementia and a 71 percent lower risk of vascular dementia, caused specifically by cerebral atherosclerosis (hardening of the small arteries to the brain).

In a 1998 article in the *Journal of the American Geriatrics Society,* Thomas Obisesan and his colleagues reported that moderate wine consumption was associated with decreased odds of developing macular degeneration, a common cause of age-related vision loss and blindness. They suggested that when promoting activities directed at improving cardiovascular health, particularly in recommending moderate wine drinking, this too may help reduce the rate of blindness among older people.

With respect to human kidney stone and gallstone diseases, Gary Curhan and his associates at the Brigham and Women's Hospital in Boston, Massachusetts, found a 59 percent decrease in risk for kidney stone

THE RISKS OF ALCOHOL

In general, alcohol consumption is associated with a higher risk of stomach ulcers and gastric bleeding, but there is a difference between wine and other alcoholic drinks in this effect. An interesting study by Inger Bak Andersen and her colleagues at the Danish Epidemiology Science Centre at Copenhagen University Hospital, Denmark, reported in 2000 that alcohol drinkers who reported at least 25 percent of their alcohol consumption as wine were four times less likely to have serious bleeding stomach ulcers. Sensibly pairing food with wine is certainly safer than other alcohol drinking habits.

formation by drinking an eight-ounce serving of wine every day. Adolfo Attili and his colleagues in the gastroenterology section of the University of Rome report that moderate alcohol intake can protect against the formation of gallstones.

Alcoholism Is Not Responsible Drinking

Alcoholism is distinct from responsible, moderate wine drinking. The latter is healthy; the former is unhealthy and destructive. Not enough could ever be said about the dangers of drinking alcohol to excess. At the same time, we cannot ignore the benefits to improved public health that are seen with moderate and responsible wine drinking. The cost of managing cardiovascular disease in 2005 was estimated at about $241.9 billion by the American Heart Association. These costs are rising year by year. Wine is less likely to be abused than beer and spirits and, in moderation, reduces the incidence and severity of cardiovascular disease.

Moderate wine consumption is usually defined as no more than two 5-ounce glasses of wine daily for men, and one glass for women. Women are allotted less than men because of their smaller body size and relative deficiency of alcohol dehydrogenase, the enzyme that breaks down alcohol in the bloodstream. For these reasons, women are more susceptible to intoxication than men and may be at greater risk for alcohol-related injury.

A NOTE OF CAUTION: A person with a history of alcohol abuse should not drink wine or any other alcoholic beverage. A person with a bleeding disorder, a stomach problem such as peptic ulcer disease, a liver disease, or other chronic disease, should consult his or her doctor before drinking wine. Many medications are labeled not to be taken with alcohol, and wine is an alcoholic beverage. Caution should be exercised when taking medications and drinking wine. You should consult your physician or pharmacist. Most medications, however, can safely be taken while drinking wine.

THREE

NUTRITION 101: THE DIET-HEALTH CONNECTION

Human-like creatures have existed on this planet for as long
as four million years, and for roughly 99 percent of this time,
they were hunters and gatherers. . . . This means that when we're sitting
down to lunch, our stone-age bodies "expect" to be fed the same
types and ratios of fat that nourished our cave-dwelling ancestors.
When we eat French fries cooked in partially hydrogenated
vegetable oil instead of wild plants, or wolf down a fat-laden
hamburger heaped with mayonnaise instead of meat from a lean,
free-ranging game animal, our bodies register the insult.

ARTEMIS P. SIMOPOULOS AND JO ROBINSON,
THE OMEGA DIET

Health and Diet: What Is Old Is New Again

As a cardiologist, I am faced with the tragedies of cardio-vascular disease each day. Preventing heart disease and its consequences is, for me, a very real professional ambition. The role of diet in the origin of heart disease, as well as of other diseases in our modern society, has been studied extensively for more than a century. While the relationship between elevated serum cholesterol and coronary heart disease has been established for decades, the role of a healthy diet in the prevention and treatment of coronary heart disease, along with other modern diseases, is a story that is just unfolding.

The 1980s—When Low Fat Was Prime Time

As recently as the mid-1980s, nutritional experts questioned whether changes in diet could prevent coronary heart disease. Support for a low-fat diet, which came to dominate current nutritional thought, began in 1984 with the publication of the results of the landmark Lipid Research Clinics Coronary Primary Prevention Trial. In this clinical study of otherwise healthy Americans, cholestyramine, a cholesterol binder, was given to subjects over a period of seven years. Cholestyramine reduced serum cholesterol by about 10 percent and mortality by a widely publicized 24 percent. The statistics, however, may be misleading. Although the findings are significant, the absolute decrease in mortality was far less impressive: 2 percent in the placebo (no drug) group and 1.6 percent in the treated (drug) group.

Despite persistent uncertainty about the importance of these findings, leading health authorities concluded that lowering cholesterol is essential to preventing heart disease. This was later supported by numerous clinical trials of statins, drugs of much greater cholesterol-lowering potential, which are shown to reduce serum cholesterol by 30 percent to 50 percent, and produce much more dramatic reductions in heart attack and cardiac death rates.

The low-fat, high-carbohydrate diet fervently promoted by the U.S. Department of Agriculture, the National Cholesterol Education Program, the National Institutes of Health, and the American Heart Association was one of America's most extensive public relations campaigns and convinced the medical profession, as well as the public, that avoiding dietary fat is a key element in preventing coronary heart disease.

Supermarket shelves from then on have supported a superfluity of packaged goods—cookies, cakes, ice cream, nearly every food product you can think of—marked and advertised as "low fat." The message was, Eat all the low-fat foods you want; they're safe and healthy. However, many of these low-fat foods, eaten by an unsuspecting public, are dangerously high in carbohydrates, devoid of essential nutrients, and prepared with saturated fat and trans-fatty acids, which sustain the high rates of coronary heart disease and cancers that Americans now experience in alarming numbers.

The message is not just about low fat. Lowering serum cholesterol also remains a key objective in preventing heart disease and improving public health. The low-fat diet, illustrated by institutional food pyramids taught to our elementary school children and to our nation's thought leaders in university nutrition programs, may well have played an unintended role in the current epidemics of obesity, lipid abnormalities, type 2 diabetes, metabolic syndromes, and coronary heart disease.

Obesity in America: An Epidemic

Nearly two thirds of Americans are overweight, and one in three is obese. The percentage of young people who are overweight has more than tripled since 1980, with over nine million people under age 20 considered overweight.

The tragedy of this national epidemic contributes to a higher risk of most common medical conditions, such as coronary heart disease, hypertension, stroke, hyperlipidemia, type 2 diabetes, cancers, sleep apnea and other respiratory problems, gallbladder disease, and osteoarthritis.

A complex mix of genetics and environment can explain our national weight gain. Whereas obesity may be affected by a strong genetic predisposition, the genetic makeup of any population does not change quickly, and this large increase in the prevalence of obesity must therefore reflect nongenetic (that is, environmental and behavioral) factors. In general, being overweight or obese results from an imbalance in energy, meaning that we consume too many calories and do not get enough physical activity.

Metabolism, which varies from individual to individual and is dependent on many fundamental human factors, may significantly modify energy need. Highly processed foods and food ingredients, such as simple sugars and starch, require little metabolic work to digest, unlike whole grain foods and fresh vegetables, which stimulate metabolism. Whole grain foods and fresh vegetables have been underrepresented in the modern American diet, and this has likely contributed to the obesity epidemic. White bread and other offending starches begin their breakdown to simple sugars as soon as they enter the mouth. Enzymes in the mouth rapidly convert the starches to sugars; the sugars dissolve and are easily absorbed for processing into fat.

Our environment has changed at a speed that evolution cannot adapt to. Historically, humans evolved to crave sugar and fat at a time when food was scarce and quick energy was needed from these high-energy food sources to be physically active in the fight for survival. In the modern world, unlike the Paleolithic landscape of our hunter-gatherer ancestors, we have an abundance of low-priced, high-calorie foods, drive-up and drive-through restaurants, low-quality fast food, and overprocessed frozen food—and we regard these as life's conveniences.

> We are living in a world today where
> lemonade is made from artificial flavors and
> furniture polish is made from real lemons.
> ALFRED E. NEWMAN

We're plagued with low-physical-impact jobs and recreational activities. We live with powered transportation, television, computers, video games, and remote control—all of which cause us to be less active. Plato said, "Lack of activity destroys the good condition of every human being, while movement and methodical physical exercise save it and preserve it."

We crave high-calorie foods that are available to us 24 hours a day, 7 days a week. And it is how effortlessly we satisfy this craving that is making us fat. The Center for Human Nutrition at the University of Colorado Health Sciences Center has reported that the average adult gains one to two pounds of weight every year.

Behavior, including how we eat, what we eat, and how our food is prepared, as well as how we pursue physical activity, can play a large role in determining whether we are overweight or lean. This may be our greatest opportunity for intervention in the battle for weight loss and better health. The first goal in The Plan is *no more weight gain*.

Already two millennia ago, the Greeks were eating a delicious diet as healthful as any we know in the world. Instead of playing sorcerer's apprentice, we have to look at Mother Nature and see what people have been doing for thousands of years.

PROFESSOR SERGE RENAUD

CRAIG'S TESTIMONIAL

I've been an athlete all of my life. I played high school and college football, and now at age 55 and at least partly retired, I've joined a golf club and try to play three to five rounds of golf a week. I play tennis with some competitiveness and work out on occasion. I also love to eat. My favorite piece of equipment at the club is the vending machine. I became fat, and it was very unnatural for me. I also developed what my doctor called metabolic syndrome, a triad including high cholesterol, high blood pressure, and diabetes. This really frightened me. My father recently died from a stroke at age 90, and I didn't want the same to happen to me before I reached 60.

My downfall, I was certain, was my obsession with Coca-Cola. I'd drink at least six cans a day, as well as other fast foods and sweets. My car was my second dining room table. I consulted with my doctor and changed my diet. The soda disappeared instantly, and I began to eat tons of vegetables. I was allowed some wine at night, and that was a luxury. I found that eating out was doable, finding some creative Asian grills that made tasty vegetable and chicken dishes that I liked. I made it through "men-o-paunch" and lost my gut. I stopped taking blood pressure medications, and can now easily and naturally control my blood sugar, though I still take a cholesterol pill. I'm back to being lean and confident.

The Case for a Mediterranean Diet

Several important studies examining the incidence of coronary heart disease around the world have demonstrated that there is a significantly lower incidence in Mediterranean Europe. Mediterranean emigrants to the Western world who assimilate and adopt a Western diet have increased rates of coronary heart disease.

A Mediterranean diet can be difficult to define, since the region includes the cultures of at least 16 countries where a lower rate of coronary heart disease is attributed to a healthy diet and lifestyle. A specific Mediterranean diet, however, has been identified by the seminal investigator of this phenomenon, Professor Serge Renaud, in his studies of the Greek island of Crete.

Crete boasts the lowest rate of coronary heart disease and greatest longevity reported by the World Health Organization. The good health of the inhabitants of this Mediterranean island has been attributed to their diet, which surprisingly includes substantially more fat than the prudent American diet. This fat, however, is taken almost entirely as olive oil. The islanders eat more bread too, but it is exclusively of the whole grain variety.

The Cretan diet contains a minimum of animal fats and seed oil; daily intake of unrefined cereals; an abundance of fruits, nuts, legumes, and vegetables; and moderate intake of dairy products, usually in the form of cheese or yogurt. Cretans enjoy wine with their food and consume a moderate amount of fish. Snails, undeniably unpopular in the United States, are loved by the Cretans and prepared in many inventive ways as a uniquely healthy specialty. The snails of Crete naturally feed off the great variety of nutritionally rich greens found on the island. These greens contain large amounts of alpha-linoleic acid (ALA), an omega-3 fatty acid that considerably reduces the risk of heart disease.

Olive oil is an important source of fat and nutrients in a Mediterranean diet. Extra-virgin olive oil contains high levels of oleic acid, a monounsaturated fatty acid. Monounsaturated fatty acids resist oxidation, and from this we gain important benefits in better health and more graceful aging. Olive oil also boasts a range of important micronutrients, including flavonoids, carotenes, alpha-tocopherol (vitamin E), coenzyme Q, and polyphenolic antioxidants, that contribute to the heart protection benefits of a Mediterranean diet.

Juan Ruano and his colleagues in Cordoba, Spain, studied the effect of virgin olive oil, a major constituent of the diet of Mediterranean Spain, on blood vessels. They found important antioxidant, anti-inflammatory, and antithrombotic effects, as well as improved endothelial function with enhanced integrity of the inner lining of blood vessels. It is well known that these effects increase the ability of the human vascular system to resist atherosclerosis, particularly in persons with high cholesterol levels. These same salutary properties are also known to boost resistance to cancers, infections, arthritis and other inflammatory disorders, and other common diseases.

Fatty Acids

A fatty acid is an organic compound composed of a long chain of carbon atoms plus a terminal carboxyl group, which is a specific group of atoms at the end of the molecular chain that imparts its acidic properties.

Saturated fatty acids, such as palmitic acid (one of the most common saturated fatty acids found in animals), can raise cholesterol and increase the risk of heart attack and other diseases. Unsaturated fatty acids are similar in structure, except that they replace one or more single bonds between carbon atoms in the chain ($-CH_2-CH_2-$) with a double bond ($-CH=CH-$). A single double bond makes a monounsaturated fatty acid; acids with more than one double bond are called polyunsaturated fatty acids.

Polyunsaturated fatty acids, such as docosahexaenoic acid (DHA) and eicosapentaenoic acid (EPA) found in fish oils, lower cholesterol and are critical to health. Omega-3 fatty acids, which have a double bond located at the third carbon–carbon bond from the end of the fatty acid chain, are essential and defend against heart attack, cancers, and other diseases.

Omega-3 Fatty Acids

Omega-3 fatty acids are required for human health and resistance to disease, especially cardiovascular disease. Since they cannot be manufactured by the body, they are essential in the human diet. The body can easily make saturated fatty acids or monounsaturated fatty acids with a double bond at the omega-9 position, for example, but it does not have the enzymes to introduce a double bond at the omega-3 or omega-6 position. As a result, these fatty acids must be obtained from food sources; hence, they are "essential."

The modern Western diet has sacrificed much-needed omega-3 fatty acids in favor of omega-6 fatty acids. These two essential fatty acids have lived in fragile balance since the beginning of human life. The tip in the delicate balance from omega-3 fatty acids to omega-6 fatty acids in the Western diet has led to the prevalence of the many diseases that plague modern society worldwide.

Ten thousand years ago, before the agricultural revolution, human beings consumed about equal amounts of omega-3 and omega-6 fatty acids. Over the past 150 years, this balance has been upset. Current estimates indicate that Western cultures consume an omega-6 : omega-3 fatty acid ratio of 10–20 : 1 instead of 1–4 : 1. This dramatic shift has resulted in serious, deleterious health consequences.

COMMON SOURCES OF OMEGA-3 FATTY ACIDS

- **Fish.** Atlantic salmon and other fatty cold-water fish (including both Atlantic and Pacific herring, sardines, Atlantic halibut, bluefish, tuna, and Atlantic mackerel), and lake trout. These are good sources of DHA, EPA, and marine-based omega-3 fatty acids.
- **Plant.** Canola oil, flaxseed, flaxseed oil, walnuts, almonds, and leafy green vegetables such as purslane, spinach, and broccoli. These are good sources of ALA, the plant-based omega-3 fatty acid.

UNCOMMON SOURCES OF OMEGA-3 FATTY ACIDS

- **Cheese.** Alpine cheeses from animals that free-graze on high alpine greens.
- **Meat.** Wild-grazing animal meats, such as venison and buffalo. These are a source of omega-3 fatty acids and a healthy alternative for people craving meat.
- **Enhanced food.** Eggs and breads enriched with omega-3 fatty acids.

The essential fatty acids are important to the human immune system and to regulation of blood pressure. They are used to make compounds like prostaglandins and other biologic products that function like hormones and act as chemical messengers within the cells where they are synthesized. The brain is also highly enriched in derivatives of linolenic and alpha-linoleic acids. Changes in the levels and balance of these fatty acids caused by a Western diet of processed food and high-intensity agriculture have been associated with depression and behavioral changes. Altering one's diet to more natural food is associated with a reduction in abnormal behavior and an increase in attention span.

In the 1970s, scientists made one of the first associations between omega-3 fatty acids and human health while studying the Inuit, an Eskimo people of Greenland. As a group, the Inuit suffered far less from certain diseases (coronary heart disease, rheumatoid arthritis, diabetes mellitus, and psoriasis) than European populations, despite the fact that their diet was very high in fat from eating whale, seal, and salmon. Researchers eventually realized that all these foods are rich in omega-3 fatty acids, which provide real disease-countering benefits.

Omega-3 fatty acids have been shown to play a role in keeping cholesterol levels low, stabilizing arrhythmia (irregular heartbeat), and reducing the incidence and severity of inflammatory diseases such as arthritis. We now understand that ALA, one of the omega-3 fatty acids, is particularly beneficial in protecting against heart and blood vessel disease, including stroke and heart attack. A diet rich in omega-3 fatty acids reduces the incidence of asthma and serious skin diseases, such as psoriasis. Omega-3 fatty acids have also been shown to be of benefit in the management of ulcerative colitis, systemic lupus erythematosus and other autoimmune disorders, multiple sclerosis, and major depressive disorders.

Clinical studies, such as the Lyon Diet Heart Study (see Chapter One), which increased ALA omega-3 fatty acids in the diet of heart attack victims, support the vital role that these fatty acids play in the prevention and management of cardiovascular disease, particularly coronary heart disease. Omega-3 fatty acids are an important component of a heart-healthy and disease-resistant diet such as that presented in The Wine Lover's Healthy Weight Loss Plan.

ALA is found in the fats and oils of canola, flax, wheat germ, and soybean, in nuts such as walnuts, and in wild greens such as purslane, a common green in the diet of Crete. (Watch for this green to make an appearance in the near future at your local greengrocer.) Edible wild plants are a rich source of ALA, in addition to vitamins C, E, and other antioxidant vitamins. Because it is widely used in salad and cooking oils, margarines, and other foods, canola oil is a major source of ALA for Americans. The body converts ALA into longer-chain omega-3 fatty acids such as DHA and EPA, which also occur naturally in fatty fish such as salmon, herring, sardines, and mackerel. Eating fish just once a week can reduce the risk of death from coronary heart disease by as much as 50 percent, as reported in 2005 by Dariush Mozaffarian and his colleagues at the Harvard School of Public Health in the heart journal *Circulation*.

Canola Oil:
The Right Alternative to Other Vegetable Oils

Canola oil is a healthy source of ALA. One tablespoon of canola oil provides the recommended daily intake of ALA for women and 80 percent of that for men. Canola oil, which is called rapeseed oil elsewhere, has been used in cooking for centuries in many parts of the world. Before 1971, rapeseed oil was not healthy due to a high concentration of erucic acid, nor was it readily available in the United States. Breeding of rapeseed varieties in the 1960s in Canada, however, resulted in a product low in erucic acid, so that by 1978 all rapeseed oil produced in Canada was of the healthy variety, leading the Canadian government to change the name of this variety to "*can*ola oil."

Canola oil is a healthy, polyunsaturated oil that can be used as a salad or vegetable oil. It is often blended with other oils to produce nonhydrogenated margarine. As one of the best sources of alpha-linoleic acid, canola oil is an easy way to increase omega-3 fatty acid intake in one's diet.

Good and Bad Cholesterol

The healthiness of the Mediterranean diet is ascribed to its beneficial effect on the lipid profile, that is, lowering total cholesterol and bad cholesterol (low-density lipoprotein, or LDL) and raising good cholesterol (high-density lipoprotein, or HDL), as well as protecting against oxidative injury. Saturated fats, such as those found in meats and common shortenings, raise total cholesterol as well as LDL, while polyunsaturated and monounsaturated fats lower both total cholesterol and LDL. Polyunsaturated fats, such as omega-6 linoleic acid, also lower HDL and can make LDL more likely to become oxidized. Oxidized LDL increases the potential for atherosclerosis, one reason why a standard low-fat diet may fail to prevent heart disease progression and death.

Omega-3 fatty acids, such as ALA, can raise HDL, lower triglycerides, and prevent LDL from being oxidized, thus preventing atherosclerosis. Foods and oils rich in omega-3 fatty acids have such a salutary effect on the lipid profile that they are paramount to good health. Wild greens, olive and canola oils, and flaxseed are great sources of omega-3 fatty acids.

> Wherever flaxseeds become a regular food item
> among the people, there will be better health.
>
> MAHATMA GANDHI

Whole Grains Do More for You Than You Think

Whole grains, such as wheat, oats, and rice, are a source of carbohydrates, protein, and essential fatty acids. They provide a valuable combination of micronutrients, antioxidants, and phytochemicals, including minerals (calcium, magnesium, potassium, phosphorus, selenium, manganese, zinc, and iron), vitamins (especially vitamins B and E), polyphenolic compounds, phytoestrogens (lignans), and fiber. These reduce the risk of cardiovascular disease and other chronic disorders.

A diet including healthy cereals and whole grain products has additional beneficial roles in health and weight management. Whole grains are strongly associated with a reduced risk of heart attack. The often-cited Nurses' Health Study of more than 87,000 women initiated in 1976 by a collaborative research group in Boston, Massachusetts, surveyed the eating habits of study participants for more than 10 years. The researchers found that increased intake of whole grains was associated with a 30 percent reduction in coronary heart disease. An even lower coronary risk was found with bran products in particular. Whole grains tend to be digested and absorbed slowly. This slow digestion reduces insulin demand, an important factor in diabetes, weight loss, and obesity.

This concept is illustrated by the Glycemic Index (GI), a system that ranks foods by their effect on blood sugar levels. Low-GI foods produce a gradual rise in blood sugar that's easy on the body, while high-GI foods cause blood sugar as well as insulin levels to spike. The immediate release of insulin resulting from high-GI food intake causes dramatic swings in blood sugar and drives the buildup of fat in body tissues. Low-GI foods appear to ward off heart disease, prevent type 2 diabetes, avert the serious side effects of diabetes, and curb appetite (so they also help with weight loss).

A healthy diet supplemented with whole grains has been associated with a reduced incidence of hypertension and stroke and reduced serum cholesterol levels. A study of school-age children reported by Cora Tabak and her colleagues at the National Institute of Public Health and the Environment in the Netherlands showed that whole grains, as opposed to refined grains, protect against asthma. Consumption of whole grains is associated with a reduced risk of various types of cancer, type 2 diabetes and insulin sensitivity, bowel disorders, cataracts, and other pathological conditions. A diet that includes whole grains and healthy cereals is consistently associated with weight loss, and in children it can begin to protect against adult obesity.

A University of Georgia study of the awareness of the health benefits of whole grain foods showed that even though awareness of the health benefits of whole grains is high, the intake of whole grains compared to refined grains in the diet is low. In the contemporary Western diet, the majority of grain products consumed are highly refined. Refinement of grains separates the bran (outer layer) and germ (inner layer) from the starchy endosperm (middle layer) during milling, which leads to the loss of many of the beneficial nutrients and fiber.

Data from a cardiovascular disease study in Norwegian counties conducted from 1977 through 1983 showed a reduction in total mortality rates (all causes of death) from eating whole grain breads. About four times as much whole grain food is eaten in Norway as in the United States. However, many refined grain breads have recently been introduced in Norway, raising concern about a potential increase in the incidence of heart disease and other diseases.

Heart Disease Prevention Must Start in Childhood

Preventing heart disease assumes that one is able to intervene at a time before heart disease actually occurs. Unfortunately, by the time people decide that they need to pay attention to their risk of heart disease—because of their family history of early heart disease or because of the onset of well-publicized cardiac risk factors, such as hypertension, diabetes, high cholesterol levels, and smoking—it is too late to prevent a disease process that is already underway.

In a study by Steven Nissen and his associates at the Cleveland Clinic, victims of fatal motor vehicle accidents were studied to detect the earliest signs of coronary heart disease by passing small ultrasonic cameras into the heart; the object was to determine the suitability of the heart for transplantation. Surprisingly, 25 percent of the potential heart transplant donors under the age of 25 already had clear evidence of atherosclerotic coronary artery disease. The prevalence of atherosclerosis was 50 percent in the group between ages 25 and 40, and 70 percent for those over age 40.

Preventing heart disease and its consequences is accomplished by modifying risk factors. Genetic risk is not modifiable; if your parents and siblings have suffered from heart disease at an early age, the likelihood that you too will suffer from heart disease is increased, and this should alert you to correct your modifiable risks. Major modifiable risk factors include smoking, hyperlipidemia (particularly high cholesterol and triglyceride levels), diabetes, and hypertension. Other risk factors include obesity, stress, depression, and nutritional deficits.

More Evidence of the Benefits of the Mediterranean Diet and The Wine Lover's Healthy Weight Loss Plan

In 1980, Anzel Keys reported the results of the Seven Countries Study, which analyzed the causes of death and the impact of coronary heart disease spanning 25 years in discrete populations from Italy, the former Yugoslavia, Spain, Finland, the Netherlands, the United States, and Greece. Inhabitants of the Mediterranean countries experienced better health and longer life than the non-Mediterranean countries. Two Mediterranean populations from Greece were included in the study. The inhabitants of Crete had the lowest average mortality, and death from coronary heart disease was almost unheard of there.

A 2003 report by Dimitrios Trichopoulos and associates in the *New England Journal of Medicine* examined the effect of adherence to a Mediterranean diet, not smoking, physical exercise, and moderate alcohol consumption on coronary heart disease and cardiac death in men and women between the ages of 70 and 90. Adherence to a Mediterranean diet was scored by evaluating the ratio of monounsaturated (good) to saturated (bad) fats in the diet, as well as the amount of legumes, nuts, and seeds; grains; fruit; vegetables and roots; meat and meat products; dairy products; and fish. The study showed that adherence to a Mediterranean diet is associated with a lower risk of death from all causes and a 39 percent reduction in death specifically from coronary heart disease. Adding the positive effects of not smoking, regular exercise, and moderate alcohol consumption, the study concluded that 64 percent of cardiovascular deaths could have been prevented.

A Mediterranean diet featuring olive oil, vegetables, fish, fruits, and low in saturated fats and enjoyed for many years by the people of that region [Greece] is healthy and promotes longevity.

DIMITRIOS TRICHOPOULOS, M.D.,
HARVARD SCHOOL OF PUBLIC HEALTH

On the whole, a Mediterranean diet provides a natural environment for the body's tissues and organs to support longer life and disease-free living. The effects of a Mediterranean diet are also extremely quick, which means better health within days; this is because most people have a relative deficiency of alpha-linoleic acid and other key nutrients.

Can Americans Adopt a Mediterranean Diet?

Populations not accustomed to a Mediterranean diet have little problem following such a diet. The Mediterranean Eating in Scotland Project studied the effect of an Internet-based lifestyle modification program that promoted the key elements of a Mediterranean diet to healthy university students in Glasgow. Participants received nutritional information over the Internet with personal dietary feedback. Nonparticipants were given brochures on healthy eating.

The active participants increased their intake of fruits, vegetables, and legumes. They favorably adjusted their ratio of unsaturated to saturated fats, raised their HDL (good cholesterol), and thereby lowered their total cholesterol.

This innovative program, among others promoted in northern Europe, shows real promise that a Mediterranean diet can be adopted by health-conscious individuals; it also shows how such a diet can be adopted by individuals otherwise unaccustomed to it.

In a study at Harvard Medical School, 61 overweight men and women were given one of two weight loss diets: a standard low-fat diet or a Mediterranean diet that included moderate consumption of healthy mono-unsaturated fats from olive oil, olives, nuts, and nut products. Both groups consumed the same number of calories. After six months, the participants had about the same amount of weight loss. After 12 months, however, a greater number of the Mediterranean diet group who had stuck with the program maintained their weight loss. Many of those on the low-fat diet did not stick with it; not only had they regained their lost pounds, but they weighed even more than they did before starting the diet program. This is a common problem in restrictive diets, where poor adherence is often further corrupted by binge eating.

This study shows that motivation and compliance are difficult to sustain in any weight loss program. It does demonstrate, however, that a Mediterranean diet that allows people to enjoy tastier foods, including some of their favorites, in reasonable portion sizes, leads to better health, a leaner body, and sustained results.

If there is anything out there in the world
that looks like a diet that would work for a lot of people,
I think it's the Mediterranean diet.

ANDREW WEIL, M.D.,
PROFESSOR OF MEDICINE, UNIVERSITY OF ARIZONA

FOUR

WINE 101: THE JOY OF WINE

For me, winemaking always feels new; every turn
of the seasons metaphorically represents a lifetime.
Every year renews your faith, your youth, your hunger
to learn, and it teaches you forgiveness. If you listen quietly
and simply allow nature to take its course, you can be
a part of the miracle of wine.

GREG BROWN, WINEMAKER,
T-VINE CELLARS, CALISTOGA, CALIFORNIA

*W*ine is a distinctive, living beverage that has been enjoyed through the ages. With a swirl of the glass, wine creates a dance of color, a bouquet that excites the nose, and a thrill of flavor on the palate. We enjoy the beauty of time in the bottle, unleashed into the glass at this very moment, delighting so many of our senses and our sybaritic pleasures. Wine is history and occasion preserved for later indulgence. Unlike lifeless rock frozen in space, wine evolves, with maturation and change that allow development of its greatest potential at a later time.

Exciting Sights and Smells

Aromatic compounds in the wine rearrange themselves during the aging process and develop color and scents that add interest and excitement. Pigments degrade to their basic organic compounds and reorganize to form a changing palette of color. Unique flavors present themselves for a brief period, then disappear. This can be quite a surprising development. For example, the Rieslings of the Watervale, in South Australia, develop a momentary petroleum bouquet about five years after bottling. It is distinct and unsuspected, and it hardly affects the taste of the wine. To an untrained consumer, it is obnoxious. But to the connoisseur, it is dramatic.

In the summer of 2003, I joined friends Justin Ardill, a cardiologist and Clare Valley vintner, and his wife, Julie, for dinner at the McGill Estate in South Australia. The McGill Estate is home to Grange, the flagship red wine of Penfolds of South Australia. Unique wines from the estate were paired with each of the evening's dishes. We were served an aged Riesling from Watervale, a vineyard community about two hours north of the domain, paired with smoked salmon atop shredded root vegetables. The wine was a shocker, with its distinct odor of gasoline. To my later surprise and to the obvious satisfaction of the dining Aussies, the sommelier (wine steward) described the unique and beautiful petroleum aromas that this wine boasted. The flavor of gasoline is a taste that I have since come to appreciate in Australian Rieslings, as well as those from Germany, Alsace, and the Americas. It represents an expression of the grape extracting flavors from the earth and is a tribute to patience, as white wines are seldom set aside for aging.

Rotten Grape Juice

In 1999, I met R. Michael Mondavi, the eldest son of Robert Mondavi, in Arizona. The meeting was arranged for me and my colleagues to discuss our research on the heart-health benefits of red wine. Pioneers of the California wine industry, the Mondavi family has had a long and serious interest in the science of food and wine. I was taken aback by Mr. Mondavi's remark that red wine, the healthy beverage that has complemented their Napa Valley table for decades, is simply "rotten grape juice."

He's technically accurate, I suppose. Wine is the product of the breakdown of natural grape juices or, more specifically, their fermentation by yeast, which converts grape juice sugars into alcohol. Grapes are said to be instinctive to become wine. The process of grape fermentation may begin in nature on the vine, where yeasts living naturally on the skin of the grape wait patiently until the grapes mature and their skins crack, exposing the sugar-laden pulp to the yeasts, so that the process of fermentation may begin.

The Mondavi family had defined varietal wine production in America some 30-plus years earlier and has been influential in making California a destination for great wines. Varietal wines are wines based on the character of the grape varieties used in their production, such as merlot and chardonnay. But surely you cannot dismiss the importance of the great winemaker and the heavily invested winery, with its thermal-controlled fermentation tanks, expensive oak barrels, and serene, luxurious aging rooms. The optimal character of wine is certainly revealed by great winemakers, who extract the greatest potential from the grape. The quintessential lesson from this great winemaker, however, was that wine is simple yet elegant, and nature defines wine's simple elegance.

The Simplicity of Wine

Wine is a product of the grape. Almost any plant with natural sugar, unquestionably including other fruits, can be fermented. By definition, however, fruit wines (from berries and apples, for example) are not really wine. Wine is exclusively the product of fermented grape juice.

Grapevines are vigorous plants that enjoy a struggle and have the ability to flourish anywhere. They often thrive in hostile environments. Grapevines are grown in nearly all 50 of the states, where wines of unique and different characters are produced. Even the unforgiving southern Arizona desert near Tucson supports vineyards and a small, uniquely enigmatic wine industry. Richard Erath, a well-known Oregon vineyard pioneer, has recently purchased about 200 acres of high desert land near Wilcox,

Arizona, and begun to develop his vineyard project there. He has plans to grow several varietal choices, including the characteristically warm-weather grapes grenache and Tempranillo.

Great wines, however, are produced in truly great wine-growing regions. The French have a word for it: *le terroir,* meaning "the land." This concept has become universal in wine production. Every wine producer talks about it.

A favorite place of mine to experience wine and take in the tradition of winemaking is the Barolo region of northern Italy. Cannubi, arguably one of the greatest microclimates for growing grapes in the world, is home to fourth-generation Barolo producer Serio Borgogno, my adopted Italian papa. Each season, we gaze at the vast vines of Nebbiolo, covering the hills of this historic wine area, share a deep breath, and say in unison, "Ahhh, Langhe. . . ." The microclimate of the Langhe is marked by its unique combination of land, air, weather, and good fortune. The Nebbiolo grape takes its name from the dense fog that bathes the vines each morning, *la nebbia.*

Unique microclimates exist throughout the wine world. They include the gravelly seaside soils of Bordeaux, the ancient riverfront earths of Burgundy, the terraced fields of vines overlooking the Rhône River in France and the Mosel River in Germany, the hot summer days and cool nights of Barossa and Clare Valley in South Australia, and the rolling hills and soft valley floors of the Napa and Sonoma appellations of northern California.

While *terroir* and microclimate speak to the contribution that the land and space make to the vines, much of what is fundamental to the wine we enjoy is derived from the grape varietals themselves.

In viticulture, *microclimate* includes more than geography. It encompasses the area's environment, including temperature, humidity, precipitation, and the character of the earth, which may be unique in the general environment of the growing area.

Wine as Metaphor

The character of wine speaks to the temperament of life. A chilled dry Provençal rosé in the southernmost regions of France—brilliant in peach color, floral on the nose, iced on the lips, dry as parchment on the tongue and mouth—suggests a summer day at the beach, with blistering sand under foot, the resonance of soft waves in the distance, and the sun, taking to its task, warming the hearts of families and friends sharing a day together.

A fruit-forward grenache from South Australia boasts concentrated fruit flavors, such as strawberry and pomegranate, and reflects light brilliantly in the glass with energy and strength. A glass of grenache is perfect on a wintry day when a brilliant sun is available to show off its purple hues. It may make you feel strong, selfish, and self-indulgent. Grenache has adequate alcohol potential to make it a warming wintry wine.

The character of a wine makes it more appropriate to drink in hot or cold weather. In northern Italy, Dolcetto is a perfect summer wine: Light and fruity, its flavors are restrained in the cold of winter. A Barbera is often too *hot* in summer, but warms the palate in wintry weather.

A cabernet sauvignon, spiced with the vanilla of oak barrels, thick in body, and voluptuous in structure, suggests passion, romance, love, and climax. The body and heat of the wine are palatable with each tender sip. It is no wonder that this wine pairs well with meat and rich foods with sumptuous sauces.

In addition to making foods taste better, making conversation at the table livelier, and evenings with friends and family more intimate, wine has the ability to turn a middle-aged man with a scientific mind and serious occupation into a quixotic philosopher.

So wine is basically a play of life, with all of its poetic clichés. And in its commanding way, wine imposes on its audience with vigor and enrichment.

The Vineyard

In order to produce wine, one needs a vineyard to source the grapes and a winery in which wine production is performed. The operation need not be glamorous in order to produce a good wine. Remember that wine is simple.

Before rising to prominence, many prominent vintners started out producing wines in a garage. Commercial success in the wine game often leads to expensive winemaking facilities and the complexities of large-scale production. "Garage wines" are still of great interest today to producers, collectors, and consumers alike; these wines, made by hand in small quantities, can often boast great results. A garage wine movement in Bordeaux, France recently yielded unique wines to compete with the historic chateaux of long pedigree in that area. These wines are difficult to find because of their limited production, and they are very expensive.

The best wines are those that take you through themselves
and out into another world that you could not have
gotten to on your own. Great wine has a strange subterranean
current of beauty. It is not something you can summon
from a wine; but a great wine can take you there.

TERRY THEISE, WINE IMPORTER

Wine consumers have the opportunity to enjoy outstanding wines produced by large wineries, where availability is assured. Such is the case with the Robert Mondavi Cabernet Sauvignon Napa Valley, the quintessential Napa cabernet sauvignon. Wines from smaller family wineries, often produced in the owners' homes, may be limited and more difficult to find. Acquiring these wines can require a personal trip to the winery, securing a place on the exclusive mailing list, or gaining the favor of your local wine merchant, who may set aside a few bottles for you. Although often quite expensive, some of these wines have greatness yet to be discovered and can offer a rewarding value. Such is the case with T-Vine Cellars Napa Merlot from Calistoga, California, a full-bodied wine of amazing character that matches the quality of much more expensive merlots!

Winemakers invest heavily in their vineyards and wineries. Great wines demand great grapes. The winemaking process begins in the vineyard. A newly planted vineyard is unlikely to produce fruit suitable to make a good-quality wine until its third harvest. Grapes are harvested once a year, usually in the fall. Vintners who are dependent on their vineyards for their livelihood must be patient and well financed before they can expect a return for their labor.

In order to make a small fortune in wine production,
you need to start off with a large fortune.

ANONYMOUS WINEMAKER

Nature influences the annual grape crop, giving each vintage (annual harvest) its own distinct individuality. The fruit needs to be protected from natural predators, such as birds and insects, as well as from disease, such as bacteria, viruses, and mold. This has led some producers to employ modern chemicals and pesticides to protect their investment. A worldwide movement toward organic farming and biological viticulture is allowing wines to be produced without chemical interference. A good friend had cautioned me never to buy wines produced from fields where there is no grass beneath the plants. In areas where personal visits to the vineyards are possible, you can inspect the vineyards and facilities where the wines are produced; signs of untoward pesticide use or other nonorganic practices may be obvious.

In the late nineteenth century, a widespread and deadly grape pestilence in Europe destroyed nearly all the vineyards there. The cause was a deadly root louse, phylloxera, which destroyed the root system, leaves, and ultimately the grapevine. The solution, proposed by internationally known horticulturist Thomas Volney Munson (1843–1913) of Denison, Texas, was the grafting of *Vitis vinifera* (the scientific name of the wine grape varieties) onto certain resistant native rootstocks from America. Even today, the greatest wines throughout the world are produced from grape plants, mostly of European descent, grafted onto the base plant of an American grape. This is not a fact that the Old World grape industry is quick to acknowledge. Recently, certain areas that have been historically free of phylloxera infestation, particularly in the southern hemisphere, are trying to produce pure *Vitis vinifera* wines from intact, ungrafted plants.

They may soon give us the sensory experience of wines from more than a century ago.

Water is a natural resource that undoubtedly affects a wine grape harvest. Certain wine-growing areas prohibit irrigation, and all of the water in the vineyards is dependent on nature. Chance precipitation at the right or wrong times in the growing season can affect the quality and abundance of the harvest. Whereas plenty of water is good during the summer season, too much water close to the harvest can dilute the natural constitution of the grape and damage the fruit. Water and freezing temperatures as harvest approaches can lead to hail, which has been known to destroy entire crops of wine grapes in less than a few hours. Harvest time is the most crucial moment in the wine's life cycle.

The chance combination of generous sunshine, cool nights, ample water, and good fortune can produce vintages of exceptional quality. The winemakers know just when this happens, as in 1997 in the Napa Valley and in 2000 in Europe.

Superstition may also play a deciding role. I am told that if the Fresia grape of northern Italy is harvested at full moon, the resultant wine—usually light, fruity, and dry—would be sparkling, or *frizzante*. Nature works in mysterious ways!

The Harvest, Crush, and Fermentation

Grapes are harvested either by hand or by machine. Premium wine grapes are usually harvested by hand, with careful inspection of each grape cluster. The grapes are harvested into boxes or bins and delivered to wineries in open containers called gondolas. The grape clusters are placed into a crusher-destemmer, where grape leaves and stems are removed and the grapes are crushed. Immature grapes, leaves, and stems may impart an untoward green or vegetal flavor to the wine, and dried or shriveled grapes create other "off" flavors.

Often wines produced in bulk or at lower cost are picked by machine, which lacks the careful selection of fruit taken for crush and fermentation. I've seen an interesting operation at the vineyards of Domaines des Grandes Côtes, Beychac-et-Caillau, Bordeaux, that employed a device that vibrates the vine in such a way that only the mature grape berries are released and collected for wine production. It is an inventive technology that appears to be quite effective.

Ultra-premium wines, which are of the highest quality and expense, are produced with such great care that each berry going into the wine is carefully inspected. Incomplete maturation or even minor bruising of a grape lands it in the reject pile. Handling of the grapes is kept to a minimum, and crushing, rather than beneath the feet of family and friends or under the stainless steel auger of modern crushers, is left to a softer, gentler exposure of the grapes to their natural weight in the fermenter. This process is known as whole-berry fermentation. Such is the case with Opus One, an ultra-premium red wine produced in the Napa Valley by the partnership of the Robert Mondavi family (Robert Mondavi Winery) of Napa and the Baron Philippe Rothschild family (Château Lafite Rothschild) of Bordeaux.

If the grape juice produced by the crush is destined to become white wine, it is quickly separated from the skins. Yes, red grapes can, and often do, produce a white wine. The sparkling white wines of Champagne, France are traditionally produced from three grape varieties: chardonnay, Pinot Noir, and Pinot Meunier, the last two being red grapes.

The degree of color extracted into the wine is a function, in general, of how much time is spent early in fermentation in contact with the skins. Whereas a blush wine may spend only hours in contact with the pigment-laden skins, the most austere of red wines spend weeks bathing in the must of skins and seeds. These impart not only color, but also the bioactive pigments, tannins, and antioxidants that give red wines their healthful advantages over white wines.

After fermentation is complete, the juice (now young wine) is pressed from the must, racked clear, and put in oak barrels for aging. (Racking is the important process of transferring the wine between vessels to remove unwanted sediment.) In general, extreme pressing of the must is avoided, since it yields undesirable, astringent flavors. On occasion, only a single press (free run) is taken for high-end wines.

Wines, particularly red wines, are transferred to oak barrels, where they continue their development until bottling. White wines remain in stainless steel tanks for clarification before bottling.

The must—remnant seeds, skins, and yeast debris—is often discarded or repopulated into the vineyard fields as a nutrient. Sometimes, vintners send the must remaining after fermentation to a distiller, who produces a liquor of high alcoholic content, such as *grappa* in Italy, *marc* in France, and *eau de vie* in Switzerland. Red wine may be racked frequently during barrel aging to produce a clearer wine. In many wines of this type, clarity is a desirable quality.

White wines and rosés usually do not spend any time in oak and can be released early for consumption. Some white wines, such as California chardonnay, are fermented in oak and may be aged for richer flavor.

Aging the Wine

Red wines are often aged in oak barrels for several years; this allows the wine to mature before release and to achieve a level of balance before drinking. The barrels are usually made from French or American oak, although chestnut and other woods are sometimes used. Oak imparts a vanilla flavor to the wine, which many wine drinkers find quite agreeable. Vanillin and related organic compounds derived from the oak staves (the planks used to construct the barrel) have been described as catnip for humans. New barrels impart a stronger flavor to wine than reused barrels.

Wines aged in oak barrels crafted from American oak are known to be bolder in flavor than those aged in barrels from French oak. This is a distinguishing characteristic that gives perceptive wine tasters the ability to discern an American red wine from a French one.

Certain grape varieties age better in French oak; an example is the Pinot Noir, which is typically a more delicate wine and thrives in the softer character of the French-oak barrels. Bold American cabernet sauvignons most often are aged in new American-oak barrels. Some winemakers mix American and French oak barrels, as well as new and reused barrels, in a vintage. This mix of characters allows them more control over the final taste of the wine.

During construction, a partially assembled barrel is placed over a small wood fire and the inside of the barrel is charred, or "toasted." The amount or depth of toast in the barrel has an effect on the wine aged in it. Winemakers can normally order their barrels with Light Toast, Medium Toast, or Heavy Toast. The toast decision is based on the grape variety to be aged in the barrel, as well as on the style of wine to be produced.

In general, wines aged for a longer time in oak, particularly smaller oak barrels, and particularly new oak barrels, cost more; these may be designated reserve wines.

After barrel aging and prior to bottling, some wines are fined and filtered to help stabilize and clarify them. In fining, gelatin, egg white, or special clay is added; this carries suspended particles with it as it settles to the bottom. Many wines are not fined or filtered, so as to preserve more of what is natural from the grape and from the process of fermentation.

Bottling

Wines are bottled before release, then allowed to rest. This is the final stage before the slow and relatively lengthy aging process in the bottle. Wines are bottled in a sterile environment and sealed with a natural cork, man-made cork, or screw cap.

Wine bottles, labels, and closures are a part of the packaging of wine and, not to anyone's surprise, may account for a wine's popularity as much as the quality or value of the product.

Cork is harvested from the bark of the cork oak tree (*Quercus suber*), and is a renewable resource. The cork oak, found predominantly in the Mediterranean region, flourishes in many climates and has a lifespan exceeding two hundred years. Portugal and Spain produce more than 50 percent of the world's cork, which has been the traditional closure for fine wine bottles.

Since cork is a living organic product, quality and character may vary, depending on the same factors involved in the harvesting of grapes, such as plant/tree maturity, weather, and timing. Keeping wines stored in humid environments is important to prevent the cork bottle closures from dehydrating and allowing air to enter the bottle, which would oxidize or spoil the wine. As a cork ages, this may happen even in an efficiently climate-controlled cellar.

Cork also has been implicated in the spoiling of wines by imparting the flavors of trichloroanisol (TCA), a contaminant that may be integral to the cork. TCA contamination can also come from barrels or even

THE SHAPE OF THE BOTTLE

There are traditional bottle shapes for certain wines. The high-shouldered Bordeaux bottle, most common in the southeastern Bordeaux region, is most popular for bottling cabernet sauvignon, merlot, and Malbec, as well as the white sauvignon blanc and Sémillon.

The slope-shouldered Burgundy bottle, wide at the bottom and tapered at the neck, is common in Burgundy, France. This type is also used to bottle wines produced from traditional Burgundian grapes grown around the world, such as Pinot Noir and chardonnay.

The tall Hoch bottle is used in Germany (green for Mosel wines and brown for Rhine wines), as well as in Alsace (in northeastern France). It is used by wineries in many parts of the world for the traditional German grape varieties, including Riesling, gewürztraminer, and Müller-Thurgau.

The Albesia bottle, named for Alba, a historic village in the Piedmont hills, is used to bottle the traditional Nebbiolo wines of Barolo and Barbaresco, as well as Dolcetto and Barbera. The bottle guarantees the authenticity of the wine and defines the area of origin.

As younger winemakers break with tradition, new and creative bottle shapes emerge, deviating from customary shapes and allowing more individual expression and definition.

The indentation found in the bottom of most "better" wine bottles is called a punt. A punt adds strength to the bottom of the bottle, notably important with sparkling wine. Today modern glass technology allows bottles to be made that do not require a punt for strength, yet many consumers equate the presence of a punt with higher quality in sparkling and still wines.

from wood within the cellar. Although TCA does not pose a health risk, it may impart disagreeable aromas or flavors to the wine. This has given rise to alternative bottle closures, such as plastic corks, screw tops, or even more extreme alternatives like boxed wines (actually, an effective way to protect the natural character of the wine). These alternative closures are becoming more common. Wine enthusiasts around the globe, however, are distressed. Resolute in preserving the cork, they see the cork method of closure as "traditional," adding to the general romance, sophistication, and authenticity of the wine.

Several years ago, in advance of current trends, Patrick McGrath, M.W. (Master of Wine), a leading wine importer in the U.K., offered me a bottle of trendy New Zealand sauvignon blanc, pale in color and well chilled. He unscrewed the bottle with a twist and a snap of the wrist, proclaiming that this was the sound of wine to come. I was, of course, doubtful.

The wine industry estimates that as many as 3 percent to 7 percent of all wines have TCA contamination at levels that can be detected by consumers. Many fine wines, particularly white wines, are now closed with a screw top to protect against contamination. Traditionalists will likely continue to resist alternative closures, particularly for age-worthy red wines. One can, however, appreciate the efficiency of screw tops in preserving the character and freshness of white wine, and this may eventually come to be more broadly accepted as a closure method for other wines.

The Color of Wine

The White Wines

White wines seem to have the greatest appeal to the average American consumer. Chardonnay, a traditional French varietal from Burgundy, is the most popular wine in the United States and has been produced with great skill and craft in the Americas, notably in California's Napa Valley.

White wines are produced from white grapes or yellow to pale, straw-colored grapes, or from red wine grapes separated from their skins immediately after the crush. In general, they are fermented and aged briefly in stainless steel and released within a year. Chardonnay, particularly in California, is often fermented and aged for a time in oak barrels to give added structure and complexity.

Less likely to benefit from cellaring, white wines are most often enjoyed when young. Young white wines preserve the floral flavors of the grape and are often more acidic than red wines.

Some white wines, for example, chardonnay, may undergo a secondary fermentation process known as malolactic fermentation (also known as deacidification), in which lactic acid is created by bacterial conversion of the malic acid and which imparts a soft, buttery flavor to the wine. This process is also common in Burgundian white wines. Unlike sauvignon

WHITE GRAPES

Aligoté	Melon de Bourgogne	Sauvignon blanc
Arneis	Müller-Thurgau	Scheurebe
Chardonnay	Muscadelle	Sémillon
Chenin Blanc	Muscat	Sylvaner/Silvaner
Colombard	Palomino	Trebbiano
Folle Blanche	Pedro Ximénez	Ugni Blanc
Gewürztraminer	Pinot Blanc	Verdicchio
Grüner Veltliner	Pinot Gris/Pinot Grigio	Viognier
Malvasia	Riesling	
Marsanne	Roussanne	

blanc and other acidic white wines, American chardonnay often tries to emulate the depth and character of an austere red wine varietal.

White wines are served cold and traditionally complement fish, poultry, and lighter dishes. You will find interesting and delightful white wines to complement the many light, healthy recipes in this book.

Chardonnay, sauvignon blanc, Pinot Blanc, Pinot Gris (Pinot Grigio in Italy), Riesling, and gewürztraminer are common white varietals found on the shelves of local wineshops and supermarkets. Rieslings and gewürztraminers are often sweet, due to some residual sugar intentionally left unfermented by the winemaker. Dry Rieslings and gewürztraminers, however, may still have a sweet nose but taste dry on the palate, a result of the intense fruit flavors of the wine grape captured and preserved in the wine's bouquet. New wines on the shelves may include spicy Rhône varietals, such as Viognier, Marsanne, and Roussanne; the Austrian Grüner Veltliner; the Italian Arneis, Malvasia, and Trebbiano; and other distinctive international white wines gaining popularity on the American table.

The Serious Reds

Red wines are the most serious and complex beverages on earth. The pulp of the wine grape, as in white varieties, provides the basic constitution of the wine, but it is the soaking of the juice in the must of skins and seeds that adds the intensity of character, the uniqueness of structure,

RED GRAPES

Barbera	Grignolino	Sangiovese
Brunello	Malbec	Shiraz/Syrah
Cabernet Franc	Merlot	Tempranillo
Cabernet sauvignon	Montepulciano	Tinta Barroca
Carignane	Mourvèdre	Tinta Cao
Carmenère	Nebbiolo	Tinta Roriz
Cinsault/Cinsaut	Petit Sirah	Touriga Francesa
Dolcetto	Petit Verdot	Touriga Nacional
Durif	Pinotage	Zinfandel
Gamay	Pinot Meunier	
Grenache	Pinot Noir	

and the nuances of personality of the red wines. The great Barolo wines from northern Italy, crafted from 100 percent Nebbiolo grapes, are locally known as "the wine of kings and the king of wines."

The bathing of the wine in the must during fermentation adds tannins and pigments that allow for aging, as well as the important bioactive nutrients that create the miraculous beverage that enhances life.

Red wines vary in character, from the light and fruity Beaujolais of France and Dolcetto of Italy, to the more structured Pinot Noirs of Burgundy, northern California, and Oregon, to the dense, spicy, peppery zinfandels of the Napa Valley and northern Sonoma, to the seductive, leathery, heavily extracted cabernet sauvignons of California, the Coonawarra region in Australia, and Pauillac in France.

Like white wines, red wines extract some of their character from the earth, as well as from the components of the grape. The mineral-laden soil of Pomerol, an appellation on the Right Bank of Bordeaux, imparts a distinctive flavor of iron to the classic merlots of the region. The shiraz of Clare Valley extracts characteristic mint and eucalyptus flavors from the area's soil in South Australia. The flavor of the earth abounds most, however, in the traditional Italian wines of Piedmont and Tuscany. These distinguishing characteristics are conspicuously consistent among vintages, and they speak to the generations of winemakers who partner with nature in the vineyards, repeating the process of wine creation year after year with a variety of techniques to reproduce the characteristic style of the wine. An educated taster of fine wines can identify the wine grape, the origin of the grape, and often the vineyard location itself. The inspection of a wine's color helps to identify the age of the wine—bold and purple in youth, burnt orange to brown in advanced age.

Red wines are most often enjoyed with meats and fatty foods, since the tannins dry the tongue and merge with the fats of the meat to create an acceptable and often ideal mouth-feel. To understand the character of tannins, bite into the seeds of a simple table grape. The parchedness is also experienced by biting into a banana peel, which is also loaded with natural fruit tannins.

Blush Wines

Blush wines, or rosés, owe their lovely color to limited exposure to the grape skin and pigments. Fermented and aged in the absence of oak, these wines are most often enjoyed young, when their crisp color and fruit flavors are at their peak. Many Americans are familiar with white zinfandel, a sweet blush wine, produced from red zinfandel grapes that are fermented with limited exposure to their skins and later mixed with unfermented grape juice for sweetness. As with other sweet wines, the high sugar content of blush wines precludes a lengthy discussion, since the sugar adds calories and fat recruitment; these wines are *not* to be included in a health-conscious diet.

Serious blush wines are favored in the summer and are served ice cold (but *never* with ice cubes). These wines, common at beachside cafés on the French Riviera, are appearing more on American wine shelves and are reasonably priced. They are generally light peach in color and brilliant. The reflection of light from a young Provençal blush wine reminds me of the spectacular summer sunsets in the Arizona desert. These wines boast beautiful floral scents and are quite dry and refreshing. They are often enjoyed with light summer fare. A good blush wine complements almost any lunch menu or light dinner.

Similar dry blush wines are produced in Australia, California, and Oregon, using Pinot Noir, grenache, or—on occasion—merlot grapes.

What Price Glory?

Wines may contain flaws that alter their flavor and appeal, but in general, *a wine is good if you enjoy it.*

Price does not always indicate quality. It is always a treat to find a delicious wine that you enjoy at a bargain price. The price of wine reflects many variables, including the price of the vineyard land where the grapes are grown, the cost of human resources in wine production, the investment in winemaking equipment, and the ever-present market variables of supply and demand.

Wines from Australia and South America often present a bargain compared to their French and American contemporaries, because the cost of land is considerably less in these wine-producing areas. Interesting wines of quality and value are produced in exciting international wine-producing regions, such as the Languedoc region in southern France, the Ribera del Duero region in Spain, the Maipo Valley in Chile, and the Mendoza region in Argentina. Inexpensive Eastern European labor helps to keep the cost of wine production down in many of Europe's great wine regions.

Glorious chateaus and quixotic multimillion-dollar estates in Europe and the Americas, however, drive the prices of premium wines higher, as do the small production and intentionally limited availability of wine offered by boutique producers. Price may also reflect fabulous ratings given by reputable wine critics. For example, an average-priced Meritage red wine from California's Sonoma County more than doubled in price when, just before its release, it was given the highest ranking by a respected wine magazine.

In general, white wines are less expensive than red wines. This is because of their earlier release and absence of expensive barrel aging, with a quicker return on investment for the producer.

Buying wine is a challenging adventure, since wine labels from around the world can be intimidating. By and large, a wine label should provide all the information you need to have a basic understanding of the wine in the bottle. Bottle shape and the wine's color are the first clues to the type of wine you are considering. The content of a wine label is governed by rules and regulations that vary from country to country. The American label shows the brand name or winery where it was produced; a proprietary name given to the wine by the producer; the vintage (the year in which the grapes were harvested); the varietal (the grape variety that makes up at least 75 percent of the wine); the vineyard designation (the name of the vineyard where at least 95 percent of the wine grapes grew); the appellation of origin (the state, country, or American Viticulture Area [AVA] where at least 85 percent of the grapes grew); and the alcohol content in volume-percent. If in doubt about a particular wine, seek help from your wine merchant.

Learning About Wine
Might Just Change Your Life

The Wine Lover's Healthy Weight Loss Plan may be your introduction to the world of wine. You may find that by understanding wine, you gain a better understanding of life. You may appreciate colors, scents, and flavors more than you have in the past. And in doing so, you may appreciate art and poetry more completely. You will learn to appreciate geography, climate, and horticulture, as well as the history and cultural diversity among wine-producing regions. You will have the opportunity to meet others with similar interests and be a perpetual student of the world as you explore the world of food, wine, and food and wine pairing.

I suggest that you continue your education as follows.

- Join a local wine club.
- Spend an hour with the proprietor of your local wineshop.
- Speak to the sommelier (wine steward) at your favorite restaurant. Request an interesting bottle of wine, priced at $30 or less, to complement your meal.
- Don't be intimidated or confused by wine labels.
- Don't be shy in the presence of someone who knows more about wine than you do; consider him or her a resource.
- Subscribe to a wine magazine and read it cover to cover every month.

WINE 102:
FOOD AND WINE PAIRING

Wine—a constant proof that God loves us,
and loves us to be happy.

BENJAMIN FRANKLIN

ood and wine pairing is imprecise and extremely personal. The age-old rules of red wine with red meat and white wine with fish and fowl do not consider the range and complexity of today's ethnic foods and the creative chef's use of spices, flavors, and nontraditional ingredients. However, a basic understanding of how the components and flavors of both food and wine complement or compete with each other can greatly increase the chances of finding an agreeable harmony between wine and food.

When you first try pairing wine with food, we recommend that you start with a wine you enjoy. The good news is that if you select a wine that you enjoy, it is nearly impossible to ruin a good meal. Follow your own tastes and don't be afraid to experiment. You will find many dishes compatible with your wine choice, just as many of your favorite recipes may pair well with some unconventional wines.

Rules such as red with meat and white with fish are meant to be broken. Pinot Noir from the Willamette Valley of Oregon, a light red wine, or even a hearty Washington merlot does just fine with wild salmon caught in the Columbia River that defines part of the border between Oregon and Washington. Contrary to the experts' view, many white wine drinkers enjoy their chardonnay with liver pâté or a juicy grilled steak. Having said that, here are some general guidelines you may find helpful when looking for that perfect wine to complement your meal.

When pairing food and wine, the goal is balance. The wine shouldn't overtake the food, nor should the food mask the wine. Wine is a fundamental part of a meal; it joins the flavors of the meal. A good match brings out the nuances and unique characteristics of both the food and the wine. A memorable union of food and wine is achieved when similarities and/or contrasts of flavor, body, intensity, and taste are highlighted.

You will find that wine by itself tastes different than when it is consumed with food. This phenomenon occurs because wine acts on food much the way a spice does. Acids, tannins, and organic residues in the wine interact with the food to provide different taste sensations.

Learning about food and wine pairing makes life, and certainly cooking, more interesting. A dependable chef cooks with the same wine that he or she plans to serve with the dish. For example, the French Bœuf Bourguignon (beef burgundy) is happily enjoyed with a Burgundian Pinot Noir, just as Brasato al Barolo (braised meat in Barolo wine) is enjoyed with an Italian Nebbiolo. Some dishes may present a challenge for finding a complementary wine. Such is the case with salads and greens, a key component of The Wine Lover's Healthy Weight Loss Plan.

In General . . .

Select light-bodied wines to pair with lighter food, and full-bodied wines to go with heartier, more flavorful dishes. A delicate fish such as tilapia goes best with a light-bodied white wine, such as Pinot Gris; a heavier-bodied and oilier fish like salmon calls for a richer, fuller-bodied wine, such as chardonnay or Pinot Noir.

Mismatching a heavier wine with a light, delicate dish will overpower the dish. Similarly, a lighter wine will not even register on your flavor gauge if you match it with a hearty roast or a spicy dish.

Consider, too, how the food is prepared. Is it poached, grilled, roasted, or fried? Consider the sauces or spices that are used. For example, chicken with a citrus sauce will call for a more delicate wine than chicken cacciatore with tomato and Italian spices or a chicken breast charred on the grill. A pan-seared crab cake may stand up to a hearty red wine, such as syrah or cabernet sauvignon, but steamed crab claws with olive oil and garlic would be lost with such a wine choice.

The Science of Taste

If one can taste food, one can taste wine.
Generally speaking, what is good smells and tastes good;
what smells off and has a nasty taste is bad.
I believe this is the reason why most people are able,
correctly, to judge that one wine is better than another simply
on the basis that it tastes or smells nicer: That elementary
hedonistic judgment will fairly accurately pin down
the relative quality of the wines in question.
MICHAEL BROADBENT, *WINE TASTING*

Every human taste bud contains 50 to 100 taste receptor cells, and most people have tens of thousands of taste buds. Sweet, sour, salty, bitter, and umami—these five flavors make up the basic perceptible tastes that we experience. (Umami, the savory character in foods like mushrooms, soy sauce, and oysters, was first discovered in 1908 by a Japanese scientist who identified natural forms of glutamate, primarily from seaweed, as an indispensable and distinct taste element in Japanese cuisine.)

Salty and sour tastes in food can make wine taste fruitier and less acidic, while sweet and umami tastes can make wine taste drier and more astringent. For example, a simple cut of beef tames the tannins and brings out the fruit of a young cabernet sauvignon, but chocolate accentuates its tannins and diminishes its fruit. Asian flavors are enhanced by the fruit and floral spice of Riesling or gewürztraminer, or even a more full-bodied but naturally spiced zinfandel, whereas a merlot paired with most Asian food would be lost.

Foods that are naturally bitter, such as endive, radicchio, dandelion and mustard greens, olives, broccoli, brussels sprouts, asparagus, spinach, cabbage, kale, and dark chocolate, are all rich in dietary phytonutrients, which are essential to good health. Good cooks know how to handle bitter ingredients and flavors in creative ways, and this means using seasonings. Seasonings such as garlic, ginger, lemon, fresh or dried herbs, and salt can be used to achieve a distinguishing flavor theme and allow successful food and wine pairings. Greens simply sautéed in olive oil with fresh crushed garlic cloves and salt can accentuate the pucker of an acidic sauvignon blanc or Italian Arneis.

Take into account, too, what wine tastes like. The basic tastes of wine are sweet, bitter, and sour. Much of what we perceive as taste in wine is actually aromas. These aromas include floral, fruit, nut, vegetable, spice, herb, roasted-flavor, animal-odor, and alcohol. Alcohol adds body and makes wine feel ripe and rich.

The weight and intensity of a wine are also important factors in food and wine pairing. The weight of a wine (light-, medium-, or full-bodied) should generally match the weight of the dish. The intensity of flavors in a wine can provide contrast and be an exception to matching the weight of a wine to a dish. A sweet golden sauterne, for example, provides a balanced weight and intensity to fois gras, but also a contrast in flavors. This pairing works well, due to the strength and individuality of the wine and the dish.

Matching Flavors

Flavors are combinations of tastes and aromas, and there are an infinite number. Fine-tune food and wine pairings by matching flavors in the food and wine. Look for sweetness, acidity, or bitterness in food, and serve a

One summer I visited retired physician-turned-winemaker Al deLorimier at his northern Sonoma home and vineyard. We had lunch on the patio overlooking the beautiful vineyards. Al's wife, Sandy, prepared a tasty garden salad, full of fresh color and crispness, with greens and herbs taken earlier from her garden. They served a delightful pale yellow deLorimier Winery Sauvignon Blanc, a delicious white wine that was young and well chilled. The wine presented a characteristic grassy flavor with a sustained acidic texture that blended the many flavors of the garden salad. The coldness balanced the unevenness and astringency of the greens and was a delight! The other flavor notes in the wine included citrus, herbs, and green apple. These flavors added zest to the light meal. An example of a wine pairing that worked extremely well.

Be curious about the vineyards your wine comes from, about the people who make it, and about their gastronomy. It's often helpful to share a glass with them. I learned that afternoon that acidic foods such as salads with balsamic vinaigrette dressing, like fish served with a squeeze of lemon, go very well with wines higher in acid such as the deLorimier Winery Sauvignon Blanc.

wine that has the same characteristics. For instance, if your fish has an element of sweetness, the wine should also be sweet or floral.

Roast lamb in a rosemary sauce is well served by a red wine, such as syrah, that adds a pronounced black plum flavor. Seared steak in a pepper sauce goes brilliantly with a peppery zinfandel. A charred steak off the grill is best matched with a wine that has equal bitterness from its tannins, such as cabernet sauvignon or Sangiovese. On the other hand, tannic wines can make fish or cream flavors taste metallic. Sweetness in food can make a wine taste thin and tart if the wine is less sweet than the food.

With acidity, it is easier to think of foods that benefit from the addition of acidity in the wine selection. When you squeeze lemon on a seafood dish, consider matching the dish with a wine that has a higher acid content. Sauvignon blanc, a wine with high acidity, also complements lemon chicken, while chicken with mustard and herbs (Dijonnaise) pairs better with a chewy syrah or syrah blend.

Contrasting Flavors

Sometimes, paradoxically, contrasting flavors, rather than matching flavors, work well in food and wine pairing. This strategy is based on the notion that opposites attract, that opposite characters in the food and wine complement each other, with a pleasing outcome. Highly spiced foods and highly alcoholic wines are clear illustrations of this. The result of this combination could be too hot!

Consider a California zinfandel, with an alcohol level greater than 15 volume-percent, and Sunday afternoon chicken wings. The wine may be quite acceptable by itself, but when paired with peppers and hot sauce, you may need assistance from the local fire department to control the inferno in your mouth. A better wine choice would be a low-alcohol, fruity wine like Riesling, gewürztraminer, or Pinot Blanc, which will lower the heat of the dish. Because hot dishes can numb the palate, they often pose a challenge and make appreciating a wine difficult. Finding contrasting flavors in food and wine, however, whether intentionally or by accident, can produce a new and unexpected experience.

Food and Wine Adjustments

If your food and wine seem off balance, slight adjustments to the food are possible. The addition of a salty, acid, or sweet flavor can help bring your meal into balance.

Food that has a prominent salty, sour, or bitter taste makes a wine seem sweeter and less tannic. To compensate, you can add a touch of sweet flavors to the food. Food with a prominent sweet or savory taste makes a wine seem more tannic, less sweet, and more acidic. To overcome this, add lemon juice or a touch of salt. Adjustments like these have been done in the world's best kitchens for years, and they will work for you as well.

Sweet foods, such as tomato sauce, Japanese teriyaki, and honey-mustard glazes, make wine seem drier, so try a slightly sweet wine with lots of spices to balance the flavor. Pinot Blanc, gewürztraminer, and Riesling are good choices.

High-acid foods, such as a salad with a strong vinaigrette dressing, soy sauce, or fish served with a squeeze of lemon or lime, go well with wines higher in acid—sauvignon blanc, Pinot Gris, or Dolcetto. In general, if a dish is acidic, the wine should be acidic. Duck with orange, for example, calls for a more acidic wine than duck with olives.

Bitter and astringent foods (think a mixed-green salad of arugula, Greek kalamata olives, or grilled vegetables) accentuate a wine's bitterness such that they should be complemented with a full-flavored, fruit-forward wine—chardonnay, cabernet sauvignon, or a Bordeaux blend. Big red wines such as a zinfandel or syrah are excellent with a classic steak or lamb chops.

Natural Success in Food and Wine

Clearly, the most natural pairing of food and wine involves matching regional foods with wines produced locally. Foods specific to a geographic area tend to have an affinity for the local wines. It is no coincidence that lamb dishes, such as those of the Middle East, pair so well with the full-bodied syrah. The syrah grape, famous in French Rhône wines such as Hermitage and Côtes du Rhône and synonymous with Australian shiraz, can be traced to the city of Shiraz, Iran. Shiraz is the capital of the Fars province and is known as the city of poets, flowers, and wine.

Another example of smart regional pairing is the hearty stews of Italian hunters, or *cacciatori,* with dry red wines, such as Sangiovese-based Tuscan Chiantis and Nebbiolo-based Barolos. The Asian influences on the cuisine of the Pacific Northwest are a natural match for the Pinot Gris, Pinot Blanc, Riesling, and Müller-Thurgau produced there.

A good rule of thumb is to determine the geographic origin of the dish you're preparing, then look for wines or wine varieties that are indigenous to that area.

Wine and Cheese

Wine and cheese is such a unique experience in food and wine that it deserves special mention.

In most parts of the world, cheese is an artisanal product, made—like wine—by successive generations of producers with careful attention to details such as organic farming, animal health and well-being, and traditional craft methodology. The result is a distinctive texture and flavor that defines regional cheeses. Unlike processed cheeses common in the United States, handcrafted cheeses are bold in flavor and aroma, and they age with the grace of some of the fine wines with which they are enjoyed. In some European countries, the best wine is reserved for the final cheese course at the end of the meal.

Cheese, at first glance, may not seem to be a heart-healthy food. Since it is often paired with wines with higher alcohol content (port, for example), a health-conscious dieter may be wary. A study by Christa Hauswirth and her colleagues, presented to the American College of Cardiology in 2002, showed that cheese made from the milk of cows that graze on high Alpine pastures, where the fresh alpine grass contains high amounts of omega-3 fatty acids such as alpha-linoleic acid, provides a healthy balance of fats and can be a source of heart-protecting fatty acids.

Full-bodied red wines go well with sharp cheeses, while milder cheeses pair best with fruitier red wine. Goat cheeses pair well with dry white wine. Soft cheeses, such as Camembert and brie (if not overripe), pair well with almost any red wine.

It is certainly best to look for locally produced wines to enjoy with regional cheeses. Some suggestions include Camembert and brie with a dry French Bordeaux, Gorgonzola with an Italian Barbera, Muenster with an Alsatian gewürztraminer, Spanish Manchego with a dry Tempranillo, and American white cheddar with a Napa Valley merlot.

Cooking with Wine

Whether you add a small amount of wine to a fish-based dish or a full bottle to enrich a slowly simmering casserole, wine can transform the humblest to the most luxurious of dishes. A good rule is to use only wines that you would drink yourself. Using bad wine for cooking will undoubtedly result in a bad-tasting meal.

Some dishes call for specific wines, for example, Brasato al Barolo, a traditional dish of meat marinated in Barolo wine. Where Barolo wine is hard to find or exorbitant in price, a generic Nebbiolo or full-bodied syrah is a reasonable substitute.

When a dish calls for wine, it often requires additional liquid, such as stock or water for stews and marinated meats. Wine blends with other food flavors and, when cooked or heated, concentrates the fruit nuances in the wine, not the alcohol.

The most common use of wine in cooking is to deglaze meat, fish, and vegetables in a saucepan and to use the reduction of wine and natural food components as a sauce. The amount of time spent reducing the wine is dependent on the alcohol content and color of the wine. White wine needs to be reduced less than red wine, simply to burn off the alcohol and leave its delicate flavors with the dish. Red wine is reduced until it is almost gone, so that the color compounds are reduced, as well as the flavor. The result is a rich blend of flavor that better complements meats and darker dishes.

Serving Several Wines at a Meal

In a meal progression where multiple wines are served, serve lighter wines before full-bodied ones. Serve dry wines before sweet ones, unless a dish with some sweetness is served early in the meal, in which case it can be matched with a wine of like sweetness. Serve low-alcohol wines before high-alcohol ones.

A sparkling wine, such as Champagne or Prosecco, may begin or finish a meal. White wines should precede red wines at the table, since the body and tannins of red wine may render the palate insensitive to the flavors of a more delicate white wine.

A sweet wine often concludes a meal, although it may also pair well with an appetizer of duck liver or pâté at the beginning of the meal. Common sense, along with an understanding of the flavors, weight, and integrity of the wines to be served, provides ample guidance for a pleasant wine and food experience.

Decanting Wine

Decanting is pouring wine into another vessel, usually of clear glass crystal, before serving. Decanting is typically reserved for older red wines containing sediment that can cloud a wine and add bitterness. Wine decanters allow the wine to breathe and may improve the flavor of older red wines. Younger red wines can also benefit from the airing of their sharp young tannins, allowing easier drinkability and yielding a more pleasurable wine. White wines and everyday wines are not decanted.

Before decanting a wine, let the bottle rest upright to allow the sediment to sink to the bottom. Slowly pour the wine into the decanter, keeping the bottle at an angle so as to prevent sediment from sneaking into the decanter. When you want to make an evening special, decant. Decanting can be a great way to add glamour to a fine dining experience.

Wine Glasses and Serving

When pouring wine, fill the glass no more than two thirds full (about five ounces). This will leave ample room to swirl the wine and smell the bouquet.

As important as serving temperature is the type of wine glass in which a wine is served. The shape of a wine glass can impact the taste of the wine, and for this reason different types of wine are served in different glasses. Sparkling wine flutes are tall and thin. Still white wine glasses are generally tulip shaped and have a smaller bowl than red wine glasses. Red wine glasses are more rounded and have a larger bowl.

A suitable all-purpose wine glass should be transparent to allow the taster to examine the color of the wine and its body, and have a slight curve inward at the top to hold in the bouquet. The thinner the glass or crystal, the better. As a general rule, it is better to use a glass that is too large than one that is too small.

Enjoying the Wine

Appearance

Take a good look at the wine. Its appearance is important. It is best to view the wine against a plain white background. The color of a red wine gives a clue to the age of the wine. Many red wines start life as a deep purple color; some lose their youthful intensity and begin to take on a tawny,

TEMPERATURE FOR SERVING

The temperature at which a wine is served has a huge impact on its taste. Serving wine cool masks some imperfections and is good for young or inexpensive wines. Colder temperatures can mask sweetness in a wine, increase the perception of acidity, and accentuate tannins. Warmer temperatures allow expression of the wine's characteristics, are best with an older or more expensive wine, but may accentuate the expression of the alcohol.

Consider the following guidelines for wine temperatures at serving.

* Sparkling wines and sweet wines: 40°F to 45°F
* Dry white wines and blush wines: 50°F to 60°F
* Light-bodied (low-tannin) red wines: 50°F to 65°F
* Medium- to full-bodied red wines: 65°F to 68°F

Folio Wine Partners, a wine import and distribution firm in Napa, California, asserts that a bottle of wine will cool 4°F for every 10 minutes in the refrigerator and will warm at about this same rate when removed from the refrigerator and left at room temperature.

The best way to chill a bottle of wine is in an ice bucket, but if you need to chill a bottle of wine in a hurry, 20 minutes in the freezer works.

---

brick red hue later in life. This is most notable at the rim (surface) of the wine. Because different grapes produce wines of different color intensities, visual examination of the wine helps determine the grape variety. For example, Pinot Noir is almost always the lightest red wine on the table, whereas cabernet sauvignon, merlot, and syrah are of an inky purple to black hue.

Similar information may be gathered from inspecting a white wine. For example, a sauterne, a popular dessert wine, starts off a lemon gold color that deepens with age, turning a rich, golden amber. The color of a white wine also gives clues to the grapes used, as well as to the region where the grapes were grown. Cool-climate wines tend to have less color; for this reason, a chardonnay from Burgundy is usually paler than an Australian chardonnay. Certain grapes have a characteristic hue, for example, the green tinge of Riesling and the ivory hue of Pinot Gris.

The wine drinker often looks for fine wine to have *legs* or *tears*. These terms refer to the clear droplets of wine that run down the inside of the glass after the wine has been swirled. This reflects the alcohol level in the wine; the thicker and more persistent the legs or tears are, the greater the alcohol content of the wine.

Smell

The nose detects the typical aromas of the grape. The lightest, most fragile are aromas of flower and fruit that rise to the rim of the glass, while the center of the glass fills with green vegetal scents and earthy, mineral components. The heaviest aromas, typically of wood and alcohol, remain at the bottom of the glass. Swirling the wine in the glass stimulates these aromas by moistening a larger surface area of the glass, mixing the wine with air, and increasing the evaporation and intensity of the aromas.

Afraid of spilling? Place the base of the glass on the table and move it in a circular motion on the tabletop, thereby stimulating the wine.

Stick your nose in the glass and enjoy a good sniff. Young wines have fruity aromas that relate to the grape variety. As wines age, secondary aromas develop that may be more earthy or complex. Whereas our tongues recognize only five basic tastes, our sense of smell may identify hundreds of substances from memory or by association. Many people feel that the bouquet of a wine is the most enjoyable part of the experience, more so than actually tasting it.

Ann Noble, an enologist at the University of California at Davis, developed the Wine Aroma Wheel to provide a common vocabulary and greater accuracy in communicating what one smells in a wine. For example, if you find a wine's aroma fruity, the Wine Aroma Wheel helps you narrow your impression, perhaps to tropical fruit or berries, and then to make further distinctions—raspberries, strawberries, blackberries, and so forth.

Sipping

Take a small amount of wine in your mouth and distribute it to the different parts of your tongue to inventory the different tastes of the wine.

Allow the wine to roll all over your tongue and carefully draw a breath around it to allow the wine to mix with air on your palate. Notice the texture of the wine, or mouth-feel. A wine is balanced if it is in harmony with its components, that is, with its aroma, acid, tannin, fruit, and sweetness.

The *finish* describes the sensation in your mouth after you've swallowed the wine. The flavors may linger for a while on the palate after the wine has been swallowed, and this is referred to as the wine's *length*. The greater length a wine has, the more time you have to enjoy it, and it is true that wines of greater length are generally of better quality.

It's Subjective, After All

Always remember that, in matters of gastronomy,
no matter how hard some people may aspire,
there are no ultimate rules or arbiters. No one can point
a finger at you and say, "Thou hast sinned by serving
a Mâcon Blanc with a hamburger!" If you don't enjoy it,
you have only yourself to blame, but your guests
should be far too grateful that someone else is taking
the trouble to give them a meal to criticize.

JANCIS ROBINSON, *HOW TO TASTE*

The principles of food and wine pairing are simple: Concentrate on fresh and healthy ingredients, keep the flavors uncomplicated and complementary, and don't allow the food to overwhelm the wine (or vice versa).

Subjectivity and personal bias ultimately dominate any food and wine pairing, and this book is no exception. The recipes presented here are paired to my liking with some of my favorite wines. The pairings generally follow the simple rules outlined in this chapter. I invite you to be contrary and critical.

In addition to a selected wine, I recommend alternative varietals with each recipe. If nothing else, experimentation with food and wine pairing provides for good table conversation and lively debate.

My hope is that you experience as much delight in creating and presenting these food and wine combinations as I have in discovering them. There is nothing more genuinely pleasing to me than sharing great food, wine, and conversation at the table. I will be truly pleased if this book helps to enhance this sublime connection of mind, palate, stomach, and spirit.

SIX

THE WINE LOVER'S HEALTHY WEIGHT LOSS PLAN ... TAKES FLIGHT

A meal without wine is like a day without sunshine.

JEAN ANTHELME BRILLAT-SAVARIN

flight *n.* A series of similar wine samples tasted for subtle comparisons.

A wine flight is an especially exciting way to enjoy wine. It matches wines of similar flavors, often of the same varietal or color, or from the same geographic area. In *flight,* a row of glasses is set down, each filled with a moderate amount of a different wine. You taste them side by side and learn how they are similar and different. Flights are a great way to learn about wine and the nuances of the grape.

The Wine Lover's Healthy Weight Loss Plan is divided into three flights.

With this approach, you will learn how to change your life and enjoy your diet experience. New food flavors and textures and new wines await you. Your newly gained knowledge about healthy foods is ready to be brought together with great wine flavors. And most important, you are losing weight—and achieving continued weight loss success without compromising on taste and enjoyment.

Weight loss through diet is one of the best ways to achieve better health. To a great extent, you are genetically predetermined to be thin or heavy. Thin people become heavy and heavy people become obese when their environment cheats their genetics. They surrender to the temptation of foods high in sugars, and saturated fats disrupt nature's plan. These foods are all around us and available to us 24 hours a day, 7 days a week.

Get back to basics and reclaim your genetic potential. Let your diet bring you better health and a more positive self-image, and at the same time you are building up a resistance to heart and blood vessel diseases, as well as to other common disorders.

Focus on Freshness and Quality

People in the Mediterranean region shop frequently during the week. Their ingredients are fresh, and meals are prepared daily. They buy vegetables and fruits from farmers markets, where produce is sold that has been harvested at peak ripeness that very day. They eat what is seasonally available. For a daily supply of fresh greens and herbs, most people have small organic vegetable gardens. Foods are simple and consistent. A side of freshly pan-wilted greens prepared in minutes complements any meal. The colorful table is teeming with nature's own vitamin store, a powerhouse of disease-preventing nutrients.

More and more of our local supermarkets are stocking fresher vegetables, as well as organic foods. Find a farmers market in your area. Experiment with new leafy green vegetables. And most of all, avoid the temptation to eat what seems easy (packaged foods)—but in fact compromises your health and well-being.

Organic Foods

The U.S. Department of Agriculture considers food *organic* if it has been produced by farmers who use renewable resources and conserve soil and water to enhance environmental quality. Organic meat, poultry, eggs, and dairy products come from animals that are given no antibiotics or growth hormones. Organic food is produced without using most conventional pesticides, fertilizers made from synthetic ingredients or sewage sludge, bioengineering, or ionizing radiation.

What Does Medical Science Say About Eating Organic?

We instinctively believe that organic food is better and helps us to avoid harmful toxins that may contribute to disease. The medical literature is inconsistent, and to date, a significant benefit of organic over conventional foods has not been identified. Certified organic fruits and vegetables are expected to contain fewer chemical residues than conventionally grown alternatives, and therefore they should be healthier. In a study by Chensheng Lu and his colleagues at Emory University, the conventional diet of 23 school-age children was replaced with an organic diet for five days. Urine samples revealed a prompt and dramatic drop in urine organophosphorus pesticide residue. Organophosphorus compounds are potent toxins and, with sufficient exposure, can be life threatening.

On the other hand, organic foods may not be expected to contain fewer environmental contaminants like cadmium and other heavy metals, plant toxins, biological pesticides, and pathogenic microorganisms; these are likely to be present in food from both sources. Ulrich Kopke, a medical researcher at the University of Bonn, Germany, concludes that "organic agriculture has been confirmed as environmentally sound and more sustainable than mainstream agriculture. Related to this knowledge, the consumer's well-being is based on indulgence and the certainty that by purchasing, eating and enjoying organic food, one has contributed to a better future and an improved environment."

Plant a Garden

Planting a garden is easy. Seeds can be raised indoors in small pots or paper cups. Herb pots of basil, parsley, cilantro, chives, mint, oregano, and rosemary look great at the kitchen window and put the freshest of flavorful cooking ingredients at your fingertips. Healthy greens can be adapted to an outdoor garden or grown in pots and planters on a patio. A home garden can be a family project in which everyone benefits.

The Mediterranean Diet

We know instinctively that a Mediterranean diet is a good way to eat. *Mom always said to eat your vegetables.* The Mediterranean diet includes abundant amounts of plant foods, such as grains, vegetables, fruits, legumes (beans, peas, and lentils), and nuts.

Further, the Mediterranean lifestyle embraces a diet that includes only small amounts of meat and sweets, plus regular consumption of fish. Fats come from healthy sources, such as olive oil, canola oil, and flax, as well as the fat in fish and plants. Mediterraneans consume wine regularly with their meals. They are physically active and have an optimistic view of life, health, and family. They set aside time at midday for a family meal, and time is set aside for a siesta—for the body as well as the mind.

Many Americans living abroad report a low-stress lifestyle, which includes daily walks to the market, a midday siesta, early evening strolls with friends and neighbors, plenty of fresh fruits and vegetables, and wine with meals. The foods provide a natural abundance of monounsaturated fats and polyunsaturated omega-3 fatty acids.

So much health advice is focused on the "don'ts":
don't eat butter, don't smoke, etc. It is nice to be able to focus
on some "dos" for a change. Do eat a diet resembling
that common to the southern part of Europe.

DR. IAN GRAHAM, PROFESSOR OF EPIDEMIOLOGY,
TRINITY COLLEGE, DUBLIN

Most physicians and nutritionists now agree that the Mediterranean diet is the best way for all of us to eat and that the Mediterranean lifestyle promotes better health. The Mediterranean diet is not just about weight loss, it's about good food and a good life.

- ◆ **Do** eat more vegetables, fruits, legumes, and nuts.
- ◆ **Do** use olive and canola oil exclusively.

ITALIAN PARSLEY

Italian parsley grows vigorously when potted and given enough sunlight and water. As the world's most popular herb, parsley has many health benefits. As a source of vitamin C, it provides antioxidant protection; it also counters anemia, is a traditional diuretic, and may help kidney function and control gout. It is also a good source of folate.

Chopped parsley adds a clean and bright flavor to any dish—salad, vegetable, fish, or meat. Parsley also adds visual pizzazz and is a wonderful natural mouth freshener.

Rosemary, sage, and oregano are also easy to grow and are aromatic and prolific.

A Quick Green Side Dish

2	teaspoons extra-virgin olive oil
1 to 2	garlic cloves, crushed
8 to 16	ounces fresh greens (such as spinach, Swiss chard, and mustard, beet, or turnip greens)
1 to 2	tablespoons rice wine vinegar or balsamic vinegar, or juice from 1 lemon
	Sesame seeds, pine nuts, soy sauce, or chili flakes (optional)

Heat the olive oil in a large nonstick sauté pan over medium heat until almost smoking. Add the garlic. Toss in the greens and sauté until almost wilted, less than one minute, stirring constantly. Don't overcook. Add the vinegar or squeeze a lemon over the greens. Top with sesame seeds, pine nuts, soy sauce, or chili flakes, if desired.

Serve immediately.

- ◆ **Do** eat whole grains (instead of processed wheat flour and breads).
- ◆ **Do** drink plenty of water and a moderate amount of wine with meals.
- ◆ **Do** make time for enjoyable meals with family and friends, and treasure the family moments associated with them.

The Mediterranean Pyramid is a simple illustration of the traditional healthy dietary and lifestyle practices of Mediterranean cultures. The pyramid is based on a culmination of research dating back to the 1950s, when the studies that have been discussed in previous chapters began to reveal the most important of health facts in modern human nutrition: A Mediterranean diet that is rich in vegetables, fruits, nuts, and whole grains (base of the pyramid), that is limited in meats, saturated fats, and sweets (top of the pyramid), and that is paired with physical activity and moderate wine intake, leads to a longer life and important resistance to the common diseases that plague our modern society, such as heart disease, stroke, and cancers.

First Flight

Take these first two weeks to clean out your kitchen cupboards and try some healthful additions to your current lifestyle. The First Flight's focus is on taking a good look at healthy resources close to home and restocking your pantry with healthy ingredients, spices, and wine.

First, purge your pantry and refrigerator.

- Throw out foods containing high fructose corn syrup, processed sugars, and white flour, and foods with added sugars and sweeteners.
- Dispose of the refined white sugar (although we keep some to fill the hummingbird feeder).
- Get rid of the soda pop; limit fruit juices (and remove all juices that are not 100 percent juice).
- Throw out corn oil and blended cooking oils. (Replace them with 100 percent canola oil. Once opened, keep canola oil in the refrigerator, since it can spoil.)
- Read labels on all food packaging to detect unhealthy ingredients.
- Eliminate foods with trans fats, man-made hybrids of otherwise healthy oils that promote heart disease and cause cancer.
- Throw out the butter. (Substitute 100 percent canola margarine without trans or partially hydrogenated fats.)
- Remove sweetened cereals and instant oatmeal packets.

- Get rid of white rice and instant potatoes. (Purchase brown rice, wild rice, and whole grains as substitutes for processed starches.)
- Dispose of sauces and dressings that have added sugars and corn syrup, such as barbecue sauces and commercial salad dressings.
- Toss out anything that has been in the cupboard for more than three months; it hasn't been eaten—and likely shouldn't be eaten.

Make room at the kitchen window for herb pots, and plant some basic herbs. You can start from seed or plant small seedlings available seasonally from your local nursery or market. Parsley and basil are great herbs to start with and will come in handy for salads and vegetable and fish dishes. Your own basil makes a quick and tasty pesto or a healthy dressing for fish.

Adjust your diet.

- Eliminate ice cream, doughnuts, chips, candy, cakes, cookies, and all fast foods.

Basil and Olive Oil Dressing

Put ¼ cup of extra-virgin olive oil, a handful of fresh-cut basil, and one or two cloves of fresh garlic in a blender; blend well. Use as a dressing lightly drizzled over poached or broiled fish or over seared scallops.

Balsamic Vinaigrette Dressing

¾   cup of the best extra-virgin olive oil available
¼   cup balsamic vinegar
1   tablespoon Dijon mustard
1   tablespoon canola mayonnaise
1   teaspoon dried herbes de Provence (dried marjoram, thyme, savory, basil, rosemary, sage, lavender, and fennel seeds)

Combine the olive oil, vinegar, mustard, and mayonnaise in a small bowl. Blend vigorously with a whisk. Add the herbes de Provence. Whisk again until smoothly blended and the herbs are evenly distributed.

- Don't overeat.
- Have a salad every day, and try a homemade salad dressing using olive or canola oil, such as the delicious balsamic vinaigrette featured on page 85.
- Taste several different extra-virgin olive oils to determine your taste preferences. In general, greener extra-virgin olive oils, made from olives harvested when young, have a grassier flavor characteristic of southern France and Liguria, on the northwestern Mediterranean coast of Italy. More mature olives produce golden oil with peppery flavors characteristic of the prized olive oils of Tuscany and California.
- Satisfy your urge for starch with steamed, boiled, or broiled root vegetables, such as potatoes, yams, Jerusalem artichokes, rutabaga, turnips, carrots, and parsnips.

  Visit your local grocery and spend time in the fresh vegetable aisle. Talk to the grocer and find out what is in season and where the produce comes from. (Locally produced food is fresher.)

  Drizzle the vegetables with a bit of extra-virgin olive oil, and add salt and fresh pepper for taste. You may also puree root vegetables in a blender or food processor with minced fresh ginger; add apple or other natural 100 percent fruit juice to create a richer flavor. This delicious and filling side dish is loaded with vitamins and healthy nutrients.
- Visit the local farmers market and buy organic products and unfamiliar produce that is only available on a seasonal basis.
- Set aside time to prepare and eat meals. Preparation of a healthy meal can be short and simple. Make a plan, and share your meal with family and friends.
- Eat nothing after 8 P.M. This is an important facet of your diet, and if you are used to nighttime snacks, you must give them up. Your body winds down in the evening, and metabolism slows during sleep. You have no need for nighttime calories or energy; the calories are simply stored as fat overnight.
- Visit a local wineshop and get to know the proprietor. Examine labels, check prices, and ask questions. Attend scheduled wine tastings to experience new varietals and to increase your knowledge of wine.

EXPLORE YOUR LOCAL FARMERS MARKET

A farmers market is one in which farmers, growers, and producers from your area set up stalls to sell their produce direct to the public. Shoppers come face to face with the farmers who grow their food. Farmers markets give you the opportunity to choose produce in its natural season at the peak of flavor and nutrition. Many products are organic and have been grown, reared, caught, brewed, pickled, baked, smoked, or processed locally. It's a great source of fresh seasonal fruits and vegetables, and, especially for city dwellers, an exciting, family-friendly gathering place.

Buying the Wine

Buy three bottles of wine—two white and one red—for the first week. Buy three bottles—two red and one white—for the second week. Mix up the grape varietals. You may use the following recommendations as a guide.

WEEK ONE

Sauvignon blanc A white wine with high acidity and citrus flavors; it goes well with salads, fish, and light dishes.

Riesling A white wine with sweeter flavors; it complements spicier dishes, Asian foods, and grilled food.

Pinot Noir A light and fruity red wine, sometimes austere; it is a good match for fish, poultry, and meat.

WEEK TWO

Zinfandel A heavy, spicy, peppery red wine; it is great with meat, poultry in brown sauces, and fatty fish.

Cabernet sauvignon The king of American red wine, dry and tannic; it is best with the main course.

Gewürztraminer A floral and tangy white wine; it goes well with soups, fish, and salads mixed with nuts.

ATILLIO

Atillio directs the wine department of a large supermarket chain and has personal experience with heart disease. He had a heart attack about 10 years ago.

"I'm often asked to help choose a good wine. I enjoy giving advice. Tasting many wines is part of my job. Price is important to many of our customers. Despite what many people think, you don't need to spend a lot of money for a good bottle of wine. Great buys are available from Australia and Italy, where some of my favorites come from.

"A novice should try a lighter, fruitier red wine like a Pinot Noir from Oregon or an Italian Barbera, where there are less aggressive tannins. More adventurous consumers would enjoy a Napa Valley zinfandel or a shiraz (syrah) from South Australia, with bolder and more playful flavors. I try to steer my customers to red wines, and I'm not shy about telling them that it's good for their health, particularly their heart."

These wines will give you a sense of your likes and dislikes. Take notes. You'll soon have the opportunity to explore other wines with similar or contrasting flavors and character.

Do your homework; subscribe to a wine magazine.

Purchase satisfactory wineglasses, or select your favorites at home. Make sure that five ounces of wine occupies no more than half of the glass. Mark the glass with a wax pencil at the level of five liquid ounces, the standard serving.

Second Flight

It is time to get down to business. Preparation is over, and the diet starts now. For the next two weeks, the diet is deliberate and specific.

Stock up on the ingredients needed to satisfy this second phase of The Plan.

Make time for exercise and relaxation. Eat slowly and enjoy the food. By now, you have a healthy supply of herbs in the kitchen, and the greens are growing in the garden outside.

GREEK-STYLE YOGURT

Greek-style yogurt is available at Trader Joe's, Whole Foods Market, and other specialty food stores. If you are unable to locate Greek-style yogurt, you may thicken whole milk yogurt by following these easy instructions.

Homemade Greek-Style Yogurt (makes 2 cups)

1 quart gelatin-free whole milk plain yogurt

Line a colander or strainer with a double layer of cheesecloth. Add the yogurt, cover, and place over a large bowl to catch the liquid (whey) that separates from the yogurt. Allow to drain 2 to 4 hours at room temperature.

Discard the liquid, place the yogurt in a sealed container, and refrigerate.

NOTES The whey can be used in baking a variety of breads. The draining and thickening process reduces the yogurt by one half.

VARIATION You may place the strainer and bowl in the refrigerator for 8 to 24 hours; the longer the yogurt is allowed to sit, the thicker it becomes. It should be about as thick as softened cream cheese.

Breakfast

You have three choices for breakfast. This is your largest allotment of carbohydrates for the day.

- One cup of Greek-style yogurt, topped with ½ cup of unsweetened 100 percent whole grain cereal and a handful of berries (blackberries, blueberries, or raspberries).
- Two slices of whole grain bread (or toast), spread with extra-virgin olive oil or 100 percent canola margarine, plus one or two pieces of fresh fruit, such as apples, bananas, oranges, or grapefruits.
- Irish Oatmeal with Walnuts and Figs (see recipe on page 109).

Lunch

Salad and vegetables only—make it green! Have a large plate of salad, perhaps with raw or partly steamed green vegetables (broccoli, asparagus,

Quick and Easy Fresh Tomato Sauce

4 to 6	ripe tomatoes, seeded and chopped
1	handful of basil
1	handful of oregano
1 to 3	garlic cloves, chopped
1	tablespoon extra-virgin olive oil
	Salt and pepper

Put the tomatoes in a medium bowl. Add the basil, oregano, and garlic. Stir in the olive oil. Season to taste with salt and pepper. Let sit 20 minutes.

NOTE Mix with hot pasta and Parmesan cheese, or serve over fresh vegetables.

green beans, or peas). You may add one hard-boiled high omega-3 egg or a handful of chopped walnuts. Dress the salad with a blend of extra-virgin olive oil, canola, vinegar, and salt and pepper, or with Balsamic Vinaigrette Dressing (see recipe on page 85). You may also have steamed vegetables with Quick and Easy Fresh Tomato Sauce (see the recipe above).

Dinner

Prepare a small portion of fish or poultry, either grilled or broiled, or pan-fry a small portion of fish, poultry, or meat mixed with vegetables and spices. Garnish with fresh-cut parsley or other herbs. Add a side dish of greens or root vegetables. Have fruit for dessert.

Drink one glass of wine with dinner—your choice!

Snacking is discouraged during the day, but if you must snack, eat fresh fruit or a small handful of walnuts or almonds.

No after-dinner snacks are allowed. You are finished eating for the day.

Third Flight

By now, you have already noticed a positive change in how you feel, and you have lost some weight. You will see a significant change in your body shape, and your self-image will improve dramatically with as little as a

Quick Dinner Recipe for Two

1 to 2   teaspoons extra-virgin olive oil
   2   garlic cloves, crushed
   2   portions of fish or skinned chicken (breast or thigh)
      Splash of white wine
      Kosher salt and freshly ground pepper
   1   tablespoon fresh herbs, chopped (optional)

Heat the olive oil in a nonstick sauté pan. Add the garlic. When the oil is smoking, add the fish or chicken. Fry the fish 3 minutes on each side; fry the chicken a little longer. Add the wine and reduce the liquid to a sauce. Add salt and pepper to taste.

If you are adventurous, tip the pan after the wine is added to ignite the liquid.

VARIATION For a satisfying vegetarian meal, substitute tofu for the meat.

---

5 percent loss in body weight. If the changes have not been significant enough for you, continue the Second Flight, then slowly add new recipes and healthy food creations.

Choose from the 125 recipes in this book. Maintain the Mediterranean lifestyle you have developed. Continue to concentrate good carbohydrates in the morning, so that you can burn them off in your daily activities. There are a number of delicious breakfast options in the recipe section. Don't skip breakfast.

Continue to have salads for lunch, and make a meal of seasonal vegetables. You may add a slice of whole grain bread at lunch, topping it with up to 2 ounces of Alpine cheese or seasoned poultry or fish.

Enjoy wine with dinner.

Men may have two glasses of wine per day, women may have one.

Go, eat your bread in gladness and drink your wine in joy,
for your action was long ago approved by God.

ECCLESIASTES 9:7

GARLIC

Garlic, one of the oldest known medicinal plants, has been credited with fighting heart disease, lowering blood pressure, and helping to fight off colds. Shela Gorinstein and her colleagues at the Hebrew University/ Hadassah Medical School in Jerusalem recently reported in *Life Sciences* that raw and boiled garlic improves plasma lipid metabolism and plasma antioxidant activity.

You don't need to count calories, but eat calories that count. You don't need to count carbohydrates or fat grams either, just eat in moderation and avoid simple carbohydrates (sugars and processed white flour) and saturated fats. Eat small portions that satisfy your energy needs for the rest of the day and leave you satisfied. Remember that the equation *calories in versus calories out* influences weight gain and weight loss. Eat in moderation!

Get daily exercise, whether it be a formal workout program or simply increased physical activity fit into your day. This will help you to more easily lose weight and maintain your lower weight. Take more steps during the day, and set aside time for regular aerobic exercise.

Losing weight is a matter of retraining our bodies to the ways of earlier, simpler cultures. Wild greens, legumes, olive oil, whole grains, and wine are the ways of the Mediterranean cultures, especially that of the island of Crete in Greece. We need to let nature provide the food that enhances our survival. Natural foods enriched by the imagination of creative cooking can make simple dishes savory, tasteful, and healthy.

Beware of Greeks bearing gifts: It may just make you thin and save your life!

SEVEN

LIVING THE WINE LOVER'S HEALTHY WEIGHT LOSS PLAN

> In general, mankind, since the improvement of cookery,
> eats twice as much as nature requires.
>
> BENJAMIN FRANKLIN

Food and Lifestyle

Under the Piedmont Fog

A few years ago, to satisfy a romantic vision, my family purchased a centuries-old farmhouse in the final stage of renovation in the Langhe hills of Piedmont in northern Italy. *Piemonte* sits at the foot of the Alpine peaks, sandwiched between *Monto Bianco* (Mont Blanc) to the northwest and *Genova* (Genoa) on the Mediterranean to the southeast. With *Torino* (Turin) as its capital, *Piemonte* was recently in the spotlight as host of the 2006 Winter Olympic Games.

A gastronomic paradise, *Piemonte* is home to the ethereal white truffle and is historically linked to the origin of solid chocolate confection. The *Piemontesi* are spiritual consumers of food and wine. A *Piemontese* is an expert in food and wine by birthright. In *Piemonte,* the foods are not necessarily Mediterranean and the wines are not ordinary or conducive to everyday consumption. The Langhe region produces, arguably, the most serious red wines in the world. Yet in our *Piemonte,* lifestyle, food, and eating are heavily influenced by the neighboring Mediterranean provinces. The grand Barolo and Barbaresco wines are reserved for special occasions, and delightful table wines are produced as part of the daily tradition.

I became aware of the true value underlying The Wine Lover's Healthy Weight Loss Plan years ago after several visits to this gourmand's paradise. I happened upon this small agricultural area serendipitously while vacationing in northern Italy. As a novice wine connoisseur, visiting towns of historic wine designation in the *Piemontese* area—wines like Barolo, Barbaresco, and Asti—my first stop was the tasting room of a small family wine farm owned by the Serio Borgogno family.

Naively expecting someone to speak English and introduce me to the regimented process of tasting the local wines, I was greeted by the family and taken into their living room. They opened several wines from various vintages, and the hours passed quickly as we exchanged more information about each other than we did about the wine. They spoke no English, and I no Italian. Since *Piemonte* is a region close to France and the local dialect is a patois between Italian and French, my college French served me well and smoothed over any language barriers. A lifelong relationship was instantly created between this wine family and me. We toured the farm's cellar and sampled wines of the great vintages yet to be.

After hours of being surrounded by and succumbing to the warm hospitality, I was invited to share a meal with them, with many more bottles of wine opened. I spent three amazing days with my newly adopted family. When we parted, I was showered with gifts. I was touched forever by the warmth of this family, and the *Piemonte* was forever stamped on my soul.

My memory of the earthy wines of Barolo are so distinct that, to this day, tactile images of familial warmth and the touch of the earth unfold with each glass of Barolo I drink. In the years that followed, the openness and generosity of the wine producers in the area was infecting, and my family and I have chosen to become a part of this warm, hospitable community. *Odesso sono Langherolo.* Now I am part of the Langhe community.

Despite voracious eating during our subsequent trips to the Langhe, my wife, Melissa, and I did not gain weight. We gorged on oven-warm crusty breads, salami, and an incredible variety of cheeses (*Piemonte* is a cheese lover's paradise!) that vary from town to town. We devoured plum preserves with hazelnuts, frothy whole milk cappuccinos, fresh yogurt, and seasonal fruit for breakfast. We ate salads, or *antipasti* (an assortment of small dishes, usually vegetarian, although sometimes including *carne cruda,* the local raw meat dressed with *olio d'oliva* [olive oil] and watercress), for lunch. Simple wines, such as Dolcetto or Barbera, accompanied the midday meal. During lunch at the local *trattoria* or *ristorante,* we noticed that not a single table was without a bottle of wine.

A voluptuous multicourse dinner followed later in the evening at some of our favorite *ristoranti.* We started with an appetizer, perhaps raw vegetables with *bagna cauda* (a warm anchovy-garlic sauce). A soup followed, such as *pasta e fagioli* (pasta and beans), then a pasta or risotto dish, such as *tagliatelle* (*tajarin* in the local dialect) *al ragù* (fettuccine with meat sauce) . . . and on and on the meal would continue with numerous courses. And yet no weight gain!

Of course, there were wines to go with almost every course. These were mostly produced in a nearby village, including the patiently aged Barolo, made from 100 percent Nebbiolo grapes. Nebbiolo takes its name from *la nebbia,* the fog common in the area.

When we finally purchased our own home, eating out became less of a necessity and eating in became a treat. Now we can truly enjoy the open-air markets every day, not as spectators, but as locals searching the produce stands for interesting and fresh seasonal foods. Not surprisingly, we weighed less after our trips abroad. Our pants were not as tight, my socks wouldn't stay up. Although our meals were rich and satisfying, we found that we did not overeat. Meals favored the amazing salad ingredients and vegetables we bought every day. We learned where to purchase meat and Ligurian (arguably the finest) olive oil.

We have not abandoned the restaurants, however, and have become good friends with the owners, all of whom produce and serve their own wine. We never need to look at the wine list—or at the menu, for that matter. We discuss with the proprietor what is fresh and especially delectable and—*ecco!*—the dish is produced to perfection and served with a perfect bottle of wine.

We are now good friends with the Brezza family of Barolo, who own a local hotel, restaurant, and wine cellar. Our three-year-old Sam plays with Enzo Brezza's nephew, Pietro, who is one month older than Sam. Enzo is the winemaker at Hotel Barolo. And we are family to the Borgognos of Barolo. A photograph of us hangs in their home in Barolo, and photographs of them hang in our homes in Tucson and *Piemonte*.

In our small village, we have other wonderful neighbors with whom we share wine every time we visit. They bring seasonal vegetables from their garden for us, and in hunting season they provide fresh game. Our property provides electricity to their small hunter's cabin in the hills. We communicate through my broken but improving Italian. These are simple people, but it seems that they have naturally "green thumb" farms. They tend cows, rabbits, and chickens; the roosters have very bad internal clocks (they cock-a-doodle-doo all hours of the day). Our neighbors have beautiful vineyards, which produce an unbelievable Dolcetto: dense, ripe fruit with a level of alcohol approaching 15 percent and a beautiful inky, black-purple color. They use their hands, marked with the scars of labor in the fields, to gently hold the glass of Dolcetto to the light and quote history and legends when describing its character. Every day spent in Italy is an adventure resonating with the warmth and generosity of its people.

We try not to drive locally. We walk hilly paths through the vineyards, to town and in the towns, to neighbors, to the restaurants, to the market and vendors. Walking is a community affair—a time to visit with friends and neighbors, chat with the local vendors, and immerse ourselves in the hospitable *Piemontese* lifestyle.

Market Day

Market day brings everyone to the center of town to explore the sellers' wares. We go to market on market days even if we don't need anything. It is the highlight of the week. Streets devoid of heavy traffic are packed with tented stalls featuring shirts, sweaters, socks, brassieres, underwear, linens, shoes, everything imaginable. A hardware section offers machetes and blades for working in the fields, as well as winemaking, bottling, and corking devices for the home. Home canners sell their preserves, vendors bring olive oil from Liguria, salamis from southern Italy compete with the local smoked meats, and vendors offer fresh fish from the lakes and the Mediterranean. To the American eye, the brightly colored vegetables seem to be on steroids because of their gargantuan size. In the winter, we have chestnuts, a favorite of mine. Local farmers bring an amazing variety of cultivated and wild greens and heirloom vegetables to market—many found nowhere in an American supermarket.

There are pots and pans for sale, and there are appliance demonstrations. Of course, there is wine for tasting and buying. The market also has a cheese section, where you can find Parmigiano Reggiano and Grana Padano, then nibble your way through blue-veined Gorgonzola, buttery Fontina, tangy Asiago, and an incredible array of mild, creamy ripe and sharp cheeses, mainly from cow's milk but also from goat's and sheep's milk. Wonderful cheeses are produced in the nearby hillside villages of Bosia and Murazzano in the Alta Langa.

At 1 P.M., when the market winds down, everyone heads to the café for a cappuccino or a glass of wine. If only our lifestyle could be like this in America! This is the essence of The Wine Lover's Healthy Weight Loss Plan. All that is necessary is a subscription to commonsense eating, drinking, and living.

Make Good Food Choices

The Wine Lover's Healthy Weight Loss Plan stresses good decisions and good foods. Shop frequently. Seek out farmers markets. Buy in small quantities.

This practice is characteristically European and ensures fresh, healthful ingredients. Refrigerators are small in most European and Mediterranean households, storage enough for one to two days' worth of food. Foods are purchased from local markets, and large supermarkets are rare. Many foods are homegrown, and shopping for them is surprisingly easy in most areas. Focus on vegetables, and buy what is in season. Is there any doubt that tomatoes purchased in the summer are fresher and more nutritious than in winter? Freshness yields the maximum nutritional value from foods.

Menus across the agricultural and coastal geography of the Mediterranean are heavily influenced by seasonal availability. The local menus of the *ristoranti e trattorie* in the Langhe are monotonously similar, because seasonal foods match what is available in the fields at the time. If you see a food at the farmers market, you will usually also see it on the menu. Is there any doubt that this is the way nature meant it to be? When we are in Italy, autumn provides us with the opportunity to shop for an array of colorful vegetables, pasta with fresh porcinis, and truffles. In winter, we eagerly anticipate chestnut soup, *frito misto* (deep-fried breaded vegetables or seafood), and more truffles. Spring brings a delightful ragout of veal and carrot over the local *tajarin* pasta, enjoyed with wines of the newest vintage.

Refrain from Overindulgence

Show restraint at the table. Overeating, like overdrinking, is uncivilized.

Although a Mediterranean diet allows a liberal amount of healthy foods (salads, vegetables, whole grains, and so on), basic mathematics do apply. If you consume more calories than the energy you expend, you will gain weight. The lesson is simple: Eat less! The availability of inexpensive and low-quality foods on a 24/7 basis has poisoned our society and has made us fat. You just don't find much fast food in agricultural Europe and the Mediterranean area. Don't succumb to what is cheap and easy, but clearly unhealthy.

BODY MASS INDEX

Two out of three Americans are now overweight or obese (defined as having a body mass index [BMI] over 25), and the number is rising. You can calculate your BMI by dividing your weight in pounds by your height in inches squared, then multiplying by 703.

BMI	Weight Status
Below 18.5	Underweight
18.5 to 24.9	Normal
25.0 to 29.9	Overweight
30.0 or above	Obese

Slow Food

Eating less often entails more work and greater expense than eating more. Find healthy food resources in your community, and take time preparing your food. And certainly take time eating! The art of communal eating has been all but lost in America. Remember that something interesting or amusing always happens at the table. Sharing a meal with family and friends can be as nourishing to the mind, body, and spirit as the actual food.

A movement is afoot worldwide to counter the modern cultural shift to fast food. The Slow Food Movement was founded in 1986 by Carlo Petrini in Bra, a medieval market town in the Langhe region of *Piemonte*, with a Friday morning market famous for its cheesemongers and other local produce dealers.

Make time for meals, savor the food, eat slowly, and let your palate explore all the great flavors of your healthy meals. If you put your fork down between bites, you will eat more slowly. Your meals should become a ritual. Once this happens, you will notice that your body's natural enzymatic mechanism will signal that you are satisfied so you do not overeat.

THE SLOW FOOD ASSOCIATION

Slow Food is an international association that promotes food and wine culture and is sweeping the globe. Its initiatives include the following.

- Promoting local, seasonal, and organically grown food as an alternative to the modern fast food culture.
- Protecting cultural identities as they relate to food and gastronomic traditions.
- Promoting agricultural biodiversity and caring for the environment.
- Preserving traditional cultivation and processing techniques.
- Supporting artisans who grow, produce, market, prepare, and serve healthy food.

Low-Fat Diets
Do Not Achieve Desired Goals

The mainstream medical community has recently come to the conclusion that low-fat diets are ineffective in lowering the risk of heart disease and that they don't support consistent weight loss. This was learned in the 1970s, but has since been re-researched and re-confirmed.

TRANS FATS

Read labels and avoid foods with trans fats, saturated fats, sugars, and additives. Trans fat is created when manufacturers add hydrogen to vegetable oil, a process called hydrogenation. Hydrogenation increases the shelf life and flavor stability of foods that contain the resulting trans fats. Trans fat molecules are straight, unlike their natural precursors, and can be packed tightly together, allowing a soft or liquid oil to become a solid, more concentrated margarine. Like saturated fat and dietary cholesterol, trans fat raises the LDL cholesterol that increases the risk of heart disease.

On average, Americans consume four to five times as much saturated fat as trans fat in their diets. Although saturated fat is the main dietary culprit that raises LDL, trans fat and dietary cholesterol also contribute significantly.

The Food and Drug Administration estimates that the average daily intake of trans fat in the U.S. is about 5.8 grams per person, or 2.6 percent of the day's calories. Saturated and trans fats can be found in some of the same foods, such as vegetable shortenings, some margarines (especially the harder margarines), crackers, candies, cookies, snack foods, fried foods, baked goods, and other processed foods made with partially hydrogenated vegetable oil. Lowering intake of foods high in saturated fat also reduces the intake of trans fat, which has been associated with acute inflammation and acute inflammatory diseases, and may initiate heart attacks and cancer.

A maximum safe level of trans fat in the human diet has not been established. All health agencies recommend reducing the intake of saturated and trans fats. Any formal recommendation can be likened to the maximum allowable concentration of arsenic allowed in drinking water.

A balanced Mediterranean diet is less restrictive and allows more variability and flexibility than a low-fat diet. Studies today consistently support this type of diet for prevention of heart and blood vessel disease, cancers, and other common medical conditions, including being overweight or obese.

Foods included in the Mediterranean diet may be higher in fats, but these are unsaturated (good) fats and promote chemical benefits in support of a healthy basic biology, including natural antioxidants, anti-inflammatory compounds, and antithrombotics. The unprocessed forms that promote calorie expenditure in food metabolism support better health and disease resistance, weight loss, and weight maintenance.

Compared to low-fat diets, the Mediterranean diet is less restrictive, tastier, and more acceptable, and it therefore guarantees greater long-term compliance. This means that the results achieved and benefits gained from The Wine Lover's Healthy Weight Loss Plan are long lasting.

HIGH FRUCTOSE CORN SYRUP

Much has been written about the detrimental effects of high fructose corn syrup added to commercial foods. In general, I advise you to avoid this sweetener, which adds little nutritional value.

High fructose corn syrup is a highly refined, artificial product that is cheaper, more stable, and easier for manufacturers to use in sodas and fruit juices than white sugar. Corn syrup sweeteners make up the majority of the sweet flavors in soda, condiments such as salad dressing, sauces, ketchup, and many other products. High fructose corn syrup is not the corn syrup you buy at the supermarket for baking; it's an artificial additive.

The dangers of white sugar have been known for a long time, but now the evidence seems clear that high fructose corn syrup is even more dangerous. It promotes diabetes and weight gain, and it may be responsible for the rise in obesity in Americans and the associated increase in diabetes. The U.S. Department of Agriculture reports that Americans consume more high fructose corn syrup than white sugar. It's not surprising that the rise in obesity in America parallels the increase in the use of high fructose corn syrup as a food additive.

Show restraint, and limit snacking. Some diets that count calories or points actually allow you to squander your daily calories or points on doughnuts or other indulgent food at the expense of real nutrition. Certainly, you can eat bad foods and still restrict calories; you may even be able to lose weight. But it's not good for your body, and it's not good for your long-term health.

Reward yourself periodically with a snack of dark chocolate or dried fruit—even the occasional gelato won't throw you off track. Dark chocolate is high in antioxidants and lowers blood pressure. Dried berries are naturally sweet and are also high in antioxidants.

It is important that if you are going to indulge in sweets, do it early in the day—never after 8 P.M. or within four hours of your bedtime—and never with regularity, for that conditions your body to expect high-carbohydrate snacks.

Find the Right Shopping Resources in Your Neighborhood

Many stores popping up around the country specialize in healthy food products, whole grain foods, and organic foods at reasonable prices. Major supermarket chains must now compete with the growing popularity of these stores and offer a greater variety of unique, often organic, produce and other healthy foods.

There is also a diversity of wines available in local markets. Specialty wineshops offer a broad range of international wines at all prices, as well as personal service and wine education. Take advantage of what is available near you.

Find out what wines are produced nearby. Sample locally produced wines, and meet the producers and winemakers. Participate in scheduled wine tastings.

Discover your community's unique resources. You may pay more for foods in specialty stores, and certainly for organic foods, but if so, the price is worth it.

Eat Timely

Carbohydrates, particularly whole grains, fruits, and other natural products, can be a part of your successful weight loss program.

Concentrate carbohydrates in the morning, and don't eat after 8 P.M., especially carbohydrates and sweets.

Drink plenty of water throughout the day. Water from natural springs provides a healthy source of minerals, including calcium, magnesium, and potassium. Tap water, processed by filtration, chlorination, and demineralization, deprives the body of what natural water sources had intended for us. Purified water is treated to remove impurities and trace minerals, and distilled water contains no minerals whatsoever. Water, the most basic of dietary requirements, in the form of natural spring water coaxed from the earth, refreshes our bodies. Trace minerals strengthen our bones and connective tissues, and they support our cell biology. Pay for your water; it's worth it.

When you start to feel full at a meal, stop eating. Use your salad plate for your main course and your dinner plate for your salad.

Shop at grocery stores that offer seasonal and organic fresh fruits and vegetables. Experiment. Ask your grocer how to prepare unfamiliar foods. If it's green, it can probably be sautéed in a pan of hot extra-virgin olive oil.

Eat at the table. Avoid eating in your living room in front of the television, in your office, or in front of your computer. Don't eat in bed or in the car. Make mealtime special, a family event. Eliminate harsh distractions when eating, such as television and loud music. Extraneous or loud noises often create anxiety and stress, which make you eat faster and eat more.

If you have something else to do, do it first, then begin eating. Don't rush through a meal in order to accomplish something that can be handled at another time.

Tips

+ Keep your pantry clear of high-fat processed foods.
+ Exercise daily, but more importantly, exercise restraint at the table and refrain from snacking.

- Plan daily walks, take more steps, and consider a formal exercise plan.
- Buy a pedometer and increase your level of measured activity.
- Weigh daily. The feedback, positive or negative, may be helpful.

Making The Plan Work for You

*In Europe we thought of wine as something as healthy
and normal as food and also a great giver of happiness
and well being and delight. Drinking wine was not a snobbism
nor a sign of sophistication nor a cult; it was as natural
as eating and to me as necessary.*

ERNEST HEMINGWAY

Wine is many things. Most important, it is a complement to a meal and a complement to life.

Make wine enjoyable in your house and at the table.

Experiment; try many different wines. It is believed that younger and less expensive wines are of greater nutritional and health value than aged wines, since tannins are fuller and pigments more dense. There is no need, then, to go broke at the wineshop.

Talk about wines with friends. Share taste experiences and new finds.

Plan a wine tasting evening with friends.

BE CREATIVE

A key to your success with this diet is to strive to be creative in the kitchen. Remember that a recipe is only a guideline. Feel free to make changes. Use your palate as your guide. With a little practice, you will be able to create dishes imbued with your individual style. Notice what happens to foods during cooking and how foods interact with each other. Great cooking is the outcome of experience and trust in your judgment and intuition.

Subscribe to a wine journal; among the most popular are *Wine Spectator, Wine Enthusiast,* and *Decanter.*

Plan a trip to a local wine-producing area; meet the wine producers, sample several wines, and increase your store of wine information.

Don't be intimidated. Understanding wine is easy, but it can, in some respects, be impossible. In the small wine villages of France, Italy, Spain, and other European countries, everyone is a wine critic. Wine bridges

---

Here are some additional tips to help you cook within The Plan.

- Invest in nonstick cookware or use a well-seasoned cast-iron skillet. Use nonstick cooking spray on pans.
- Marinate vegetables, meat, poultry, and fish prior to cooking; it adds a tremendous amount of flavor.
- Marinate fish and poultry in buttermilk or yogurt to tenderize them and enhance their flavor.
- When making a stock, soup, or stew, sauté the vegetables and brown the meat before adding any liquid; this results in a richer flavor.
- Save the cooking liquid from greens and reuse it in stocks, soups, and sauces.
- Cook vegetables and meats at a low temperature for a long period of time, such as in a slow cooker or clay pot; this enhances flavors without the addition of fat.
- Poach or bake fish in vegetable stock, tomato juice, diluted wine, or fresh lime or lemon juice.
- When grilling vegetables, use condiments like pesto, balsamic vinegar, mustard, horseradish, and preserves.
- Substitute whole grains or rice for bread stuffing.
- Use whole eggs sparingly. Egg whites can replace some or all of the whole eggs in most recipes, except baking. Replace one large egg with two egg whites; two medium eggs with three egg whites.
- Substitute fruit purees, such as applesauce, pumpkin, squash, apricot, and prune, for the fat in baking recipes.
- Substitute Dutch process cocoa powder for chocolate. Substitute three tablespoons of cocoa powder for one ounce of baking chocolate (if chocolate is not the only fat in the recipe).

socioeconomic gaps, and everyone enjoys the pleasures and benefits of wine.

Each person has his or her own unique nutritional needs. There is no single way of eating that works for everyone. Personal preferences, food allergies, health concerns—all are factors that influence what type of eating patterns works best for a particular individual. The Mediterranean diet offers the perfect solution; it provides a broad, comprehensive approach to eating and living that can accommodate the dietary needs of an individual without forgoing the flavors of food.

We encourage you to explore the repertoire of recipes in this book. Not only will they help you to achieve your weight loss goals, they will allow you to experience globally inspired, creative, healthy cooking that retains the flavors and textures and reflects the heritage of indigenous produce. The recipes are not merely healthy, they are ethnically diverse and satisfyingly delicious and are as much a celebration of the pleasures of eating as they are of cooking in The Plan's style.

The Wine Lover's Healthy Weight Loss Plan is a celebration of life. It encompasses an active lifestyle, a delectable, healthy cuisine paired with vivacious wines, and sharing meals with family and friends. We hope that you have been inspired by our passionate commitment to Mediterranean foods and taste to eat healthy foods, drink delicious wines, and begin to savor life . . . and lose that weight that you have struggled to get rid of.

Ask a Frenchman why he drinks wine, and he may respond, "It makes me love life."

Ask an Italian why he drinks wine, and he may respond, "It strengthens my heart and gives me health."

Ask a Greek why he drinks wine, and he may respond, "Because it is what we do."

EIGHT

BREAKFAST

EGGS PROVENÇALE

Serves 2

1 ripe tomato
   Extra-virgin olive oil
   Sea salt and freshly ground black pepper
1 tablespoon chopped garlic
2 eggs
1 tablespoon fresh chopped thyme

Slice off both ends of the tomato and cut the tomato in half. Put the tomato halves in an 8-inch sauté pan, lightly oil them on both sides, and season with salt and pepper.

Turn the tomato halves face down. Cover and cook over medium heat until softened, about 5 minutes. Turn the tomatoes over, add the garlic, and cook for about 30 seconds.

Add the eggs to the sauté pan. Top the ingredients with chopped thyme and continue to cook until the eggs are done.

NOTE Serve with a slice of crusty whole wheat baguette.

Courtesy of Chef Ghini, Ghini's French Caffe, Tucson, Arizona

IRISH OATMEAL WITH WALNUTS AND FIGS

Serves 4

4 cups water
1 cup steel-cut oatmeal
½ cup chopped walnuts, toasted
8 dried figs, chopped
1 tablespoon flax meal

Optional toppings
1 tablespoon Greek-Style Yogurt (see page 89)
1 teaspoon real maple syrup
  Dash of nutmeg
  Dash of cinnamon

Bring 4 cups water to a boil in a medium saucepan; add the oatmeal and reduce heat to a simmer. Cook, stirring occasionally, about 5 minutes.

Stir in the walnuts. When the oatmeal begins to thicken, add the figs. Cook to desired thickness. Just before removing from the heat, add the flax meal.

Add your choice of optional toppings prior to serving.

VARIATIONS Substitute hazelnuts or pecans for the walnuts, or dried dates for the figs.

BREAKFAST BRUSCHETTA

Serves 1

1   slice whole grain bread
2   teaspoons extra-virgin olive oil, plus additional for brushing
      on bread
1   garlic clove, halved
1   small tomato, cored and sliced
      Sea salt and freshly ground black pepper
1   cup assorted wild mushrooms (portobello, oyster, shiitake)
1   cup greens (spinach, arugula, Swiss chard), cleaned and chopped
1   egg

Lightly brush the bread on both sides with olive oil. Toast the bread, then rub it with the garlic clove, reserving the garlic clove to use later.

Heat 2 teaspoons of the olive oil in a medium sauté pan over medium-high heat, add the tomato slices, and lightly cook them. Season with salt and pepper. Set aside, and cover to keep warm.

Mince the garlic clove and add it to the sauté pan along with the mushrooms. Cook for about 2 minutes until the garlic is soft and fragrant. Add the greens, and toss until wilted. Season to taste with salt and pepper. Set aside, and cover to keep warm.

Wipe the pan clean, add a bit of olive oil, and cook the egg to desired doneness.

To assemble, place the slices of tomato on top of the toast, and top with the mushroom mixture and egg.

VARIATIONS A variety of toppings can be added to this bruschetta: pesto, hummus, Gorgonzola, Parmesan, roasted garlic, mashed Tuscan white beans, roasted eggplant, or fresh basil. Use whatever leftovers you have, and be creative.

SWISS MUESLI

Serves 2

- 1 cup rolled oats
- ½ cup apple juice
- ½ cup plain yogurt
- 2 tablespoons dried fruit (cranberries, raisins, currants, blueberries, cherries)
- 2 tablespoons nuts (slivered almonds, walnuts) and seeds (sunflower, pumpkin, flax)
- 1 tablespoon honey
- ½ apple, grated
- ½ banana, mashed
-   Nutmeg (optional)
-   Cinnamon (optional)

Combine the oats, apple juice, yogurt, dried fruit, nuts and seeds, honey, apple, and banana in a medium bowl. Flavor with nutmeg or cinnamon, if desired. Cover and refrigerate for at least 2 hours or overnight.

NOTE This recipe can easily be doubled and kept in the refrigerator for use throughout the week.

VARIATIONS Substitute any seasonal berries, dried apricots, prunes, pears, papayas, or mangoes, as desired. For a crunchier texture, mix ingredients just before serving.

OATMEAL RAISIN PANCAKES

Serves 2

1   cup rolled oats
1   cup buttermilk
¼   cup whole wheat flour
1   tablespoon brown sugar
½   teaspoon baking powder
½   teaspoon baking soda
⅛   teaspoon salt
¼   teaspoon cinnamon
1   large egg
2   tablespoons canola oil
¼   cup golden raisins

Combine the oats and buttermilk in a small bowl, stirring to mix. Cover and refrigerate for several hours or overnight.

To prepare the pancakes: Combine the whole wheat flour, sugar, baking powder, baking soda, salt, and cinnamon. Mix the egg and canola oil together, and stir them into the flour mixture; add the oatmeal mixture. Gently stir in the raisins. Thin with additional buttermilk if needed.

Cook on a lightly oiled hot griddle, turning when bubbles form.

NOTE Serve with Chunky Ginger Five-Spice Applesauce (see recipe on the opposite page) or real maple syrup.

CHUNKY GINGER FIVE-SPICE APPLESAUCE

Serves 4

  4 large apples (Jonagold, Gala, Golden Delicious)
  ¾ cup apple juice or cider
  1 tablespoon minced ginger
1 to 2 teaspoons five-spice powder
    Juice of 1 lemon

Peel, seed, and core the apples; cut them into small chunks.

Place the apples, apple juice, ginger, and five-spice powder into a medium saucepan. Bring to a simmer over medium heat and cook until the apples are tender.

Mash with a wire whisk until the applesauce is the desired consistency. Season to taste with lemon juice.

SAVORY CORN WAFFLES

Serves 4

1 cup whole wheat flour
½ cup yellow cornmeal
1 tablespoon sugar
1 teaspoon baking powder
½ teaspoon baking soda
½ teaspoon salt
¾ cup buttermilk
1 large egg
1 teaspoon real vanilla extract
2 tablespoons canola oil
1 cup fresh corn, removed from the cob just before adding,
    or 1 cup frozen corn, thawed

Combine the whole wheat flour, cornmeal, sugar, baking powder, baking soda, and salt in a medium bowl.

In a small bowl, combine the buttermilk, egg, vanilla, and canola oil.

Stir the liquids into the flour mixture. Whisk just to remove lumps; do not overmix. Fold in the corn. Let the batter stand for 10 minutes.

Spray the waffle iron with nonstick spray, and cook the waffles according to your waffle iron's instructions.

NOTES Serve with real maple syrup or a chunky tomato salsa and yogurt. These waffles freeze well and are far superior to store-bought waffles.

BREAKFAST FRITTATA

Serves 4

1 tablespoon extra-virgin olive oil
1 small sweet onion, thinly sliced
1 cup wild mushrooms (shiitake, Portobello, oyster), sliced
1 red bell pepper, thinly sliced
1 small zucchini, thinly sliced
1 cup shredded fresh spinach or arugula, packed
   Sea salt and freshly ground black pepper
1 tablespoon minced fresh herbs (basil, oregano, rosemary)
6 large eggs
¼ teaspoon Tabasco
1 cup grated dry Monterey jack cheese
1 cup grated Parmesan
   Plain yogurt, as garnish

Preheat oven to 350°F.

In an ovenproof 10-inch nonstick skillet, heat the olive oil over medium-high heat. Add the onion, mushrooms, pepper, and zucchini, and sauté until the vegetables are soft, about 5 minutes, stirring occasionally. Add the spinach or arugula and cook for 1 minute. Season with salt and pepper, and stir in the fresh herbs. Remove from heat.

Whisk the eggs with the Tabasco, and stir 1½ cups of the cheese into the egg mixture.

Pour the egg mixture over the vegetables. Cook over medium heat until the eggs begin to set.

Place the skillet into the oven and cook until the top is slightly brown, about 10 to 12 minutes. Sprinkle with the remaining cheese.

Carefully loosen the frittata from the pan with a rubber spatula. Cut it into 4 wedges and garnish with yogurt.

APPLE-ONION OMELET

Serves 2

3 eggs
1 tablespoon cold water
3 drops of Tabasco
  Salt and freshly ground black pepper
2 teaspoons canola margarine
1 tart apple (Jonagold, Granny Smith), peeled, cored, and
    thinly sliced
½ small sweet onion, thinly sliced
1 teaspoon chopped fresh thyme, or ⅛ teaspoon dried
½ cup grated cheddar cheese

Preheat oven to 400°F.

In a small bowl, beat the eggs with the water and Tabasco, seasoning to taste with salt and pepper.

Melt the margarine in an 8-inch ovenproof nonstick sauté pan over medium heat. Add the apple and onion, and sauté until the onion begins to soften, about 5 minutes.

Stir in the thyme. Sprinkle the cheese over the apple mixture. Pour the egg mixture evenly into the pan and cook over medium heat until the edges begin to set.

Transfer the pan to the oven and cook for 10 to 12 minutes.

Cut the omelet in half and serve immediately.

SMOKED SALMON HASH

Serves 6

2 pounds Yukon Gold potatoes
1 pound hot-smoked salmon
1 small red onion, minced
1 tablespoon prepared horseradish
1 tablespoon coarse-grain mustard
¼ cup capers
¼ cup low-fat sour cream
1 tablespoon minced fresh thyme
  Sea salt and freshly ground black pepper
1 tablespoon olive oil
6 poached eggs
  Plain yogurt, as garnish

Put the potatoes into a large pan and cover them with water. Bring the water to a boil and cook the potatoes until tender. When the potatoes have cooled completely, peel and cube them.

Shred the salmon and place it in a medium bowl. Add the onion, horseradish, mustard, capers, sour cream, and thyme. Toss to combine, and add salt and pepper to taste; set aside.

In a large heavy sauté pan, heat the oil over medium-high heat. Add the potatoes and sauté until golden brown and crisp. Add the salmon mixture and toss to combine; heat through. Add additional salt and pepper if desired.

Divide the hash among 6 plates; top each with one poached egg.

Serve each portion with a tablespoon of yogurt as garnish.

BREAKFAST POLENTA
WITH DRIED FRUIT AND HAZELNUTS

Serves 4

4 cups water
½ teaspoon salt
1 cup polenta
½ cup golden raisins or currants
½ cup chopped hazelnuts or almonds, toasted
¼ cup dried cranberries
6 Medjool dates, pitted and chopped
1½ tablespoons honey or maple syrup
1 teaspoon minced fresh ginger
½ teaspoon cinnamon
Pinch of nutmeg (optional)

Bring the water and salt to a boil. Cook the polenta according to package directions.

When the polenta is ready, remove the pan from the heat.

Stir in the raisins, nuts, cranberries, dates, honey, ginger, cinnamon, and nutmeg, if using.

Divide among 4 bowls and serve.

AVOCADO, SHRIMP,
AND MANCHEGO CHEESE OMELET

Serves 2

2 teaspoons canola oil
¼ cup diced red bell pepper
¼ cup diced sweet onion
⅓ cup bay shrimp
1 tablespoon minced cilantro
   Salt and freshly ground black pepper
4 large eggs
4 tablespoons water
2 teaspoons canola margarine
½ cup shredded Manchego cheese (or other dry cheese)
½ avocado, sliced and tossed with lemon juice

Heat the oil in a small nonstick sauté pan, add the pepper and onion, and sauté until soft. Stir in the shrimp and cilantro; season with salt and pepper.

To prepare one omelet: Beat 2 of the eggs with 2 of the tablespoons of water. Heat 1 teaspoon of the canola margarine in an 8-inch nonstick omelet or sauté pan over medium-high heat. Pour in the egg mixture. As the mixture sets at the edges, use a spatula to gently push the cooked portion toward the center. When the eggs are almost set on the surface but still look moist, sprinkle half of the cheese over the center of the omelet, then add half of the shrimp mixture and half of the avocado slices. Lift and fold one edge of the omelet to the opposite edge, and slide it onto a warm plate.

Repeat the procedure to make the second omelet.

NINE

APPETIZERS

BRUSCHETTA WITH WHITE BEAN PUREE AND WILTED GREENS

Serves 6

1 can (15 ounces) white beans, drained and rinsed
6 tablespoons fruity extra-virgin olive oil
2 to 4 large garlic cloves, finely minced
Sea salt and freshly ground black pepper
6 cups bitter greens (escarole, Swiss chard, dandelion, broccoli rabe)
2 tablespoons red wine vinegar
6 slices whole wheat peasant bread, ¾-inch thick
1 garlic clove, cut in half

Puree the beans in a food processor or mash them well with a fork. Add 4 tablespoons of the olive oil and the minced garlic, blending well. Season to taste with salt and pepper. Set aside.

Heat the remaining 2 tablespoons of olive oil in a large sauté pan or skillet (not cast iron) over medium heat. Add the greens and cook, stirring constantly, a few minutes. Sprinkle the greens with vinegar and continue to cook until wilted.

Drain the greens in a colander. Chop them fine, but not to a mush. Season with salt and pepper.

Brush both sides of the bread slices with olive oil, then grill or broil the slices until golden and toasted on both sides. Rub the hot bread with the cut garlic, spread it with the bean puree, and top each slice with wilted chopped greens.

NOTE The beans and greens can be served warm or at room temperature.

VARIATION Add 4 ounces precooked braised, coarsely shredded beef to the greens after they have been chopped; season to taste. The richer the meat, the more assertive the seasoning should be.

Courtesy of Max Duley, Executive Chef,
Peju Province Winery, Napa, California

RECOMMENDED WINE
Cabernet Franc 2003
Peju Province Winery • Napa Valley, California

ALTERNATIVES
Cabernet Franc or *Barbera*

CROSTINI WITH GORGONZOLA, CARAMELIZED ONIONS, AND PINE NUTS

Serves 4

12 slices whole wheat baguette, ¼-inch thick
3 tablespoons extra-virgin olive oil
1 large onion, thinly sliced
2 teaspoons fresh chopped sage
2 teaspoons fresh chopped thyme
1 teaspoon balsamic vinegar
   Pinch of sugar
   Sea salt and freshly ground black pepper
2 ounces Gorgonzola cheese
½ cup toasted pine nuts

Preheat oven to 350°F.

To prepare the crostini, place the baguette slices on a baking sheet and brush the tops with 2 tablespoons of the olive oil. Bake until lightly toasted, about 5 to 7 minutes. Cool.

In a large heavy saucepan, heat the remaining 1 tablespoon of olive oil over medium heat. Stir in the onion, sage, thyme, vinegar, and sugar. Cover and cook, stirring occasionally, until the onions are very tender and starting to brown, 25 to 30 minutes. Season to taste with salt and pepper.

Spread each crostini with about 1 teaspoon of cheese, top with the onion mixture, and sprinkle with pine nuts.

Serve warm or at room temperature.

RECOMMENDED WINE
Bricco S. Ambrosio Barbera d'Alba 2004
Eredi Lodali • Treiso, Italy

ALTERNATIVES
Barbera or *Sangiovese*

MEDITERRANEAN ARTICHOKE HEARTS

Serves 4

2   packages (9 ounces each) frozen artichoke hearts,
      thawed and drained
2   tablespoons balsamic vinegar
2   tablespoons extra-virgin olive oil
2   garlic cloves, finely minced
2   teaspoons finely minced thyme
1   teaspoon finely minced fresh rosemary
½   teaspoon crushed red pepper flakes

Cut each artichoke heart in half; transfer them to a bowl. Add the balsamic vinegar, olive oil, garlic, thyme, rosemary, and red pepper flakes. Stir well and refrigerate.

To serve, bring to room temperature. Serve on toothpicks.

VARIATION   Spread on whole wheat bruschetta.

RECOMMENDED WINE
Pinot Gris 2004
Erath Vineyards • Dundee, Oregon

ALTERNATIVES
Pinot Gris or *Gewürztraminer*

CUCUMBERS STUFFED
WITH FETA AND HERBS

Serves 4

2 medium English cucumbers, peeled and chilled
¼ cup crumbled Greek feta cheese
1 tablespoon plain yogurt
1 teaspoon minced fresh oregano
1 teaspoon minced fresh thyme
½ teaspoon Worcestershire sauce
  Dash of Tabasco
  Sea salt and freshly ground black pepper
  Fresh thyme leaves, as garnish

Cut the chilled and peeled cucumbers in half lengthwise.

Scoop the cucumber seeds and centers into a small bowl. Add the feta cheese, yogurt, oregano, thyme, Worcestershire sauce, Tabasco, and salt and pepper, mixing well.

Spoon the mixture back into the cucumbers, cover with plastic wrap, and chill for at least 10 minutes.

When ready to serve, cut the cucumbers into small wedges and garnish with thyme leaves.

RECOMMENDED WINE
Napa Valley Chardonnay 2003
Stony Hill Vineyards • St. Helena, California

ALTERNATIVES
Chardonnay or *Pinot Gris*

MARINATED MOZZARELLA
WITH LEMON AND CAPERS

Serves 6

12 ounces fresh mozzarella, sliced ¼-inch thick
½ cup extra-virgin olive oil
2 garlic cloves, finely minced
½ teaspoon red pepper flakes
1 tablespoon minced fresh oregano
1 tablespoon finely minced lemon zest
½ teaspoon sea salt
½ teaspoon freshly ground black pepper
3 tablespoons capers, drained and chopped
   Juice of 1 lemon
   Fresh oregano stems, as garnish

Place mozzarella slices on a medium platter.

Heat the olive oil in a small saucepan over medium heat. Add the garlic and red pepper flakes, and heat until the garlic starts to sizzle. Remove from heat and stir in the oregano, lemon zest, salt, and pepper. Let the mixture cool to room temperature.

Stir in the capers and lemon juice. Adjust seasonings. Drizzle this mixture over the cheese.

Top with fresh oregano stems as garnish.

RECOMMENDED WINE
Napa Valley Sauvignon Blanc 2004
Rudd Vineyards • Oakville, California

ALTERNATIVES
Sauvignon Blanc or *Sémillon*

BABA GHANOUSH
(ROASTED EGGPLANT WITH TAHINI)

Makes about 2 cups

1   large eggplant (about 1½ pounds)
3   garlic cloves, chopped
¼   cup tahini (sesame seed paste)
    Juice of 1 lemon
½   teaspoon salt
1   teaspoon cumin
    Dash of paprika
¼   cup chopped parsley
½   cup toasted pine nuts
    Extra-virgin olive oil

Preheat oven to 400°F.

Cut the eggplant in half lengthwise and place it cut side down on a non-stick baking sheet. Prick the eggplant with a fork, and bake it until the eggplant is soft and begins to char, 30 to 40 minutes.

After the eggplant has cooled, scoop out the pulp and combine it in a blender with the garlic, tahini, lemon juice, salt, cumin, and paprika, pureeing until smooth. Stir in the parsley and pine nuts. Drizzle a small amount of olive oil over the top.

NOTE   Serve with Parmesan Pita Crisps (see recipe on the opposite page) or a variety of fresh vegetables.

RECOMMENDED WINE
Napa Valley Signature Shiraz 2002
Darioush Vineyards • Napa, California

ALTERNATIVES
Syrah or *Grenache*

PARMESAN PITA CRISPS

Serves 4

4 whole wheat pita breads
   Extra-virgin olive oil
3 tablespoons grated Parmesan cheese
1 tablespoon Italian seasoning

Preheat oven to 350°F.

Cut each pita bread into quarters and split. Place the pitas close together on a baking sheet, rough side down. Brush the pitas lightly with olive oil; sprinkle them with Parmesan cheese and Italian seasoning. Bake until brown and crisp, about 10 minutes.

NOTE Serve with soup, salad, or dips.

VARIATIONS Fennel, cumin, sesame seeds, red pepper flakes, or herbes de Provence can be substituted for the Parmesan cheese and/or the Italian seasoning.

RECOMMENDED WINE
Chianti Classico 2000
Castello Vignamaggio ◆ Greve in Chianti, Italy

ALTERNATIVES
Sangiovese or *Nebbiolo*

SPICY ASIAN MEATBALLS
WRAPPED IN LETTUCE

Serves 6

½ pound ground lamb
½ pound ground pork
2 green onions, finely minced
3 garlic cloves, finely minced
¼ cup minced fresh cilantro
2 tablespoons Asian chili sauce
1 tablespoon Asian fish sauce
1 tablespoon soy sauce
1 tablespoon finely minced ginger
2 teaspoons finely minced orange zest
1 teaspoon Asian sesame oil
1 head Boston lettuce
1 bunch fresh mint leaves
   Asian Tomato Salsa (see recipe on page 132)
2 tablespoons canola oil

To prepare the meatballs: In a medium bowl, combine the lamb, pork, green onion, garlic, cilantro, chili sauce, fish sauce, soy sauce, ginger, orange zest, and sesame oil, mixing thoroughly. Form the meat mixture into 30 meatballs (about 1 tablespoon each); transfer to a baking sheet lined with foil; refrigerate.

Separate the lettuce into 30 small cups. Refrigerate the lettuce and mint leaves.

The meatballs, lettuce, and mint leaves can be kept refrigerated for up to 12 hours before the meatballs are cooked for serving.

Prepare the Asian Tomato Salsa.

To cook the meatballs: Heat the oil in a large sauté pan over medium-high heat and sauté the meatballs in batches until all are cooked. Place them on a pan lined with paper towels and keep them warm in the oven.

Place the lettuce cups on a serving plate. Add a meatball to each; top with mint leaves and a tablespoon of Asian Tomato Salsa.

Serve at once.

RECOMMENDED WINE
Dry Land Shiraz 2001
Reilly's Wines • Mintaro, South Australia

ALTERNATIVES
Syrah or *Merlot*

ASIAN TOMATO SALSA

Makes 2½ cups

2 cups seeded and chopped plum tomatoes
   Juice and zest of 1 lime
1 garlic clove, minced
1 Thai or jalapeño chili, minced
3 tablespoons chopped fresh cilantro
2 tablespoons Asian chili sauce
1 tablespoon Vietnamese fish sauce
1 tablespoon finely minced ginger

Combine all of the ingredients in a small bowl.

Serve at room temperature or chilled.

NOTE The salsa will keep for up to 2 days in the refrigerator.

RECOMMENDED WINE
Pinot Grigio 2003
Saddleback Cellars • Oakville, California

ALTERNATIVES
Pinot Gris or *Riesling*

SHRIMP AND AVOCADO COCKTAIL

Serves 4

1 avocado, peeled and diced
1 cucumber, peeled and diced
Juice of 1 lime
1 cup red chili sauce
¼ cup finely diced red onion
¼ cup chopped fresh cilantro
2 teaspoons horseradish
1 teaspoon Worcestershire sauce
Dash of Tabasco
1 pound medium shrimp, cooked and peeled
1 lime, cut into wedges for garnish

To prepare the cocktail sauce, mix together the avocado, cucumber, lime juice, chili sauce, onion, cilantro, horseradish, Worcestershire sauce, and Tabasco in a large bowl.

Fold the shrimp into the cocktail sauce.

Divide among 4 martini or margarita glasses, and garnish with lime wedges.

RECOMMENDED WINE
Monterey Gewürztraminer 2004
Thomas Fogarty Cellars
Santa Cruz County, California

ALTERNATIVES
Gewürztraminer or *Riesling*

SPICY ASIAN EGGPLANT DIP

Makes about 2 cups

2 tablespoons canola oil
1 eggplant (about 1½ pounds), cut into ½-inch cubes (peel if desired)
2 tablespoons sweet chili sauce
2 tablespoons rice vinegar or white wine vinegar
2 tablespoons dry sherry
1 tablespoon minced garlic
1 tablespoon minced peeled fresh ginger
1 tablespoon hoisin sauce
4 green onions, thinly sliced
2 tablespoons soy sauce
1 red bell pepper, minced
1 teaspoon sesame oil
   Sea salt and pepper

In a nonstick wok or a large nonstick skillet, heat the canola oil over high heat until it is hot but not smoking. Add the eggplant and stir-fry over moderately high heat until it is tender and browned, 3 to 5 minutes. Use a slotted spoon to transfer the eggplant to paper towels to drain.

In the wok, combine the chili sauce, vinegar, sherry, garlic, ginger, and hoisin sauce; stir-fry the mixture for 30 seconds. Add the green onions and stir-fry for an additional 30 seconds. Add the soy sauce, bell pepper, and eggplant; stir-fry the mixture until the eggplant has absorbed most of the liquid, about 1 minute.

Remove the wok from the heat, add the sesame oil, and season to taste with salt and pepper. Toss the mixture well.

Serve warm or at room temperature.

NOTES Serve with whole wheat pita, cut into wedges, as accompaniment. The eggplant mixture may be made one day in advance and kept covered and chilled.

RECOMMENDED WINE
Viognier 2004
Anne Amie Vineyards • Carlton, Oregon

ALTERNATIVES
Pinot Blanc or *Riesling*

BLACK BEAN HUMMUS

Makes 2 cups

1 can (15 ounces) black beans, drained and rinsed
   Juice of 1 lime
2 garlic cloves, chopped
1 teaspoon ground cumin
1 teaspoon ground coriander
½ teaspoon cayenne
½ cup chopped cilantro
   Sea salt

Combine the black beans, lime juice, garlic, cumin, coriander, and cayenne in a food processor. When combined, transfer to a serving bowl. Fold in the cilantro. Add salt to taste.

NOTE Serve with baked tortilla chips or whole wheat pita wedges.

RECOMMENDED WINE
Robert Sinskey Los Carneros Merlot 2001
Robert Sinskey Vineyards • Napa, California

ALTERNATIVES
Merlot or *Syrah*

WARM MEDITERRANEAN OLIVES WITH FENNEL AND ORANGE

Serves 6

8 ounces brine-packed olives, such as Niçoise or Picholine
4 tablespoons extra-virgin olive oil
1 tablespoon chopped fresh thyme
1 to 2 garlic cloves, minced
2 teaspoons finely minced orange zest
1 teaspoon crushed fennel seeds

Rinse olives in cold water until the water runs clear. Drain well.

Combine the olives, olive oil, thyme, garlic, orange zest, and fennel in a small skillet. Cook over medium-high heat until the garlic is fragrant and the oil is hot, about 5 minutes. Remove from heat.

Cool slightly; serve warm.

RECOMMENDED WINE
Vin Gris de Cigare 2004
Bonny Doon Vineyard ♦ Santa Clara, California

ALTERNATIVES
Côtes du Rhône Rosé or *Côtes du Provence Rosé*

CLAMS OREGANTA

Serves 4

¼ cup extra-virgin olive oil
3 garlic cloves, minced
4 whole plum tomatoes, seeded and coarsely chopped
3 tablespoons roasted red peppers, minced and drained
2 tablespoons minced fresh oregano
   Freshly grated black pepper
24 small hard-shelled clams (Manila clams or cockles), scrubbed well
½ cup dry whole wheat bread crumbs
1 tablespoon finely grated fresh lemon zest
1 tablespoon minced fresh mint

In a deep 6-quart heavy pot, heat the oil over medium heat. Add the garlic and cook, stirring, until the garlic is fragrant, about 1 minute. Stir in the tomatoes, red peppers, and 1 tablespoon of the oregano; cook, stirring occasionally, until the tomatoes break down, 4 to 5 minutes. Season with pepper to taste. Add the clams, stirring well to coat; cover the pot tightly and increase the heat to medium high. Cook, stirring once, until the clams open, 5 to 7 minutes. (Discard clams that have not opened after 7 minutes.)

While the clams are cooking, toss together the bread crumbs, lemon zest, mint, and the remaining 1 tablespoon of oregano.

Divide the clams and pan juices among 4 shallow bowls; sprinkle the seasoned bread crumbs over the top. Serve immediately.

NOTE Serve with crusty whole wheat Italian bread to dip into the juices.

RECOMMENDED WINE
Domaine Meriwether Brut 1998
Captain William Clark Cuvée • Salem, Oregon

ALTERNATIVES
Sparkling White or *Sauvignon Blanc*

WILD MUSHROOM PÂTÉ

Makes 2 cups

1 tablespoon extra-virgin olive oil
¼ cup finely chopped shallots
2 garlic cloves, minced
1 pound mixed wild mushrooms (shiitake, oyster, chanterelle),
   trimmed and sliced
¼ cup dry white wine
1 tablespoon chopped fresh thyme
2 teaspoons soy sauce
¼ teaspoon sea salt
⅛ teaspoon freshly ground black pepper
½ cup chopped pecans, toasted
2 ounces goat cheese or Neufchâtel cheese, softened (optional)

Heat the oil in a large nonstick skillet over medium-high heat. Add the shallots and garlic; cook, stirring, until soft, 2 to 3 minutes. Add the mushrooms; cook, stirring, until wilted and starting to brown. Add the wine, thyme, soy sauce, salt, and pepper; cook, stirring, until the wine is nearly all evaporated, 5 minutes.

Transfer the mixture to a food processor. Process with the nuts and cheese, if using. Adjust seasoning to taste. Transfer to a serving bowl, cover, and refrigerate until set, 3 to 4 hours.

NOTE Serve as a spread on bruschetta, with pita crisps, or with fresh sliced vegetables; garnish with fresh thyme.

RECOMMENDED WINE
Napa Valley Chardonnay Carneros 2003
GustavoThrace • Napa, California

ALTERNATIVES
Chardonnay or *Pinot Gris*

GRAPE LEAVES STUFFED WITH SHRIMP

Serves 4

½ cup dry white wine
¼ cup minced green onions
3 garlic cloves, minced
2 tablespoons soy sauce
2 tablespoons hoisin sauce
2 tablespoons dark sesame oil
2 tablespoons minced fresh ginger
1 to 2 teaspoons Asian chili sauce
24 medium shrimp, peeled and deveined
12 large grape leaves (fresh or brined)

To prepare the marinade, combine the wine, green onions, garlic, soy sauce, hoisin sauce, sesame oil, ginger, and chili sauce in a small bowl; whisk together until smooth.

Put the shrimp into a separate bowl. Pour the marinade over the shrimp and marinate for at least 1 hour.

If using fresh grape leaves, soak them in cold water for 15 minutes. Drain and pat dry with paper towels. (Alternatively, if using brined grape leaves, drain the liquid, then rinse and pat dry.)

Place 2 shrimp on each grape leaf near the stem end, drizzle with marinade, then fold in the sides and roll up. Secure with toothpicks or string.

Grill for 3 to 5 minutes on each side.

RECOMMENDED WINE
David Bruce Russian River Pinot Noir 2000
David Bruce Winery • Los Gatos, California

ALTERNATIVES
Pinot Noir or *Grenache*

FIG AND WALNUT TAPENADE

Makes 2 cups

1 pound fresh figs, cleaned and stemmed, or 8 ounces dried
   Mission figs, stemmed and quartered
½ cup pitted kalamata olives
2 tablespoons olive oil
1 tablespoon balsamic vinegar
1 tablespoon capers, drained
1 tablespoon chopped fresh thyme
2 teaspoons lemon zest
1 garlic clove, peeled
⅔ cup walnuts, toasted

Combine all the ingredients in a food processor and process until almost smooth. Refrigerate until serving.

Serve warm or at room temperature.

NOTES Serve with a sliced whole wheat baguette and perhaps a slather of goat cheese. It's also excellent with beef, chicken, pork, or salmon.

RECOMMENDED WINE
Syrah Napa Valley 2002
Truchard Vineyards ◆ Carneros, California

ALTERNATIVES
Syrah or *Merlot*

SATURDAY NIGHT PIZZA
WITH CARAMELIZED ONIONS,
LEEKS, AND GORGONZOLA

Serves 6 to 8

Basic pizza dough for 4 pizzas

- 1 package active dry yeast
  Pinch of sugar
- 1 cup warm water
- 2 tablespoons extra-virgin olive oil
- 2 cups whole wheat flour
- 1½ cups all-purpose flour
- 2 teaspoons sea salt
  Cornmeal

Topping for 4 pizzas

- 3 large onions (white, yellow, red), thinly sliced
- 1 leek, thoroughly washed and chopped
  Olive oil or canola oil spray
  Kosher salt
- 2 cups shredded low-fat mozzarella cheese
- 4 tablespoons blue cheese (Gorgonzola, Stilton, Roquefort)
  (a little goes a long way)
  Freshly ground black pepper
- 1 bunch fresh arugula

Saturday morning

To prepare the basic pizza dough: Combine the yeast, a pinch of sugar, and the lukewarm water to make the yeast starter. Let stand for 5 minutes.

Combine the yeast starter, oil, whole wheat and all-purpose flours, and salt.

Knead the dough on a lightly floured surface until smooth, 3 to 5 minutes, and place in a lukewarm bowl sprayed lightly with oil; cover. Allow to rise for a couple of hours.

Punch down the dough and separate it into four pieces. Place the dough on a baking pan and cover the pieces with plastic wrap. Allow the dough to rise again for several hours (or even overnight in the refrigerator).

Saturday afternoon

To prepare the topping: Thinly slice the onions and leek and spray them with a light coating of oil. Season lightly with salt. Place in a wide skillet on low heat. Cook uncovered and stir gently until very soft and caramelized, 25 to 30 minutes. Refrigerate.

(*continued*)

Saturday night

Preheat oven to 500°F.

Preheat a pizza stone on the lower rack of the oven for 30 to 40 minutes.

To make one pizza: Put one piece of the pizza dough on a lightly floured surface, and shape it into a thin irregular circle about 10 inches in diameter. Lightly sprinkle cornmeal on a pizza peel or a rimless baking pan. Transfer the shaped dough to the peel or pan. Test to make sure it slides around easily.

Top the dough with a generous layer of caramelized onions and leeks, about one fourth of the mixture. Top with ½ cup of the shredded mozzarella and a tablespoon of crumbled blue cheese. Season lightly with kosher salt. Carefully slide the pizza onto the hot stone by pulling back with a couple of jerks on the peel or pan.

Bake the pizza until bubbly and golden on the edges, about 8 to 10 minutes.

Slide the baked pizza from the stone onto a cutting board; top with freshly ground pepper and arugula leaves. Slice into wedges and serve.

Repeat the pizza-building and -baking process for the remaining 3 pizzas, brushing the browned corn meal from the pizza stone each time before baking.

Courtesy of Dave Pramuk, Robert Biale Vineyards, Napa, California

---

RECOMMENDED WINE
Black Chicken Napa Valley Zinfandel 2004
Robert Biale Vineyards • Napa, California

ALTERNATIVES
Zinfandel or *Petit Sirah*

TEN

SALADS

MOROCCAN CARROT SALAD

Serves 4

1½ pounds carrots, peeled and cut into thin slivers or ¼-inch slices
 1 tablespoon extra-virgin olive oil
    Juice and minced zest of 1 lemon
 ¼ cup chopped fresh cilantro
2 to 3 garlic cloves, minced
 1 teaspoon ground cumin
 1 teaspoon sweet paprika
 ¼ teaspoon cayenne pepper
    Sea salt and freshly ground black pepper
 2 tablespoons chopped parsley, as garnish

Prepare an ice bath.

Bring a pot of salted water to boil and blanch carrots until al dente, 1 to 2 minutes. Place immediately into the ice bath to cool; drain well. Transfer the carrots to a medium bowl.

In a small bowl, mix the olive oil, lemon juice and zest, cilantro, garlic, cumin, paprika, and cayenne pepper. Add this mixture to the carrots, stirring to combine, and season to taste with salt and pepper. Cover and refrigerate for at least 30 minutes to allow flavors to blend.

Serve, garnished with parsley.

RECOMMENDED WINE
Tempranillo Rosé 2004
Gundlach Bundschu Winery • Vineburg, California

ALTERNATIVES
Tempranillo or *Sauvignon Blanc*

BEET, ORANGE, AND MINT SALAD

Serves 4

3 large beets
2 tablespoons extra-virgin olive oil
3 tablespoons balsamic vinegar
1 shallot, minced
  Juice and minced zest of ½ orange
2 seedless oranges
¼ cup chopped fresh mint
1 cup crumbled feta cheese
  Sea salt and freshly ground black pepper
8 ounces mixed baby salad greens

Cover the beets with water in a small saucepan, bring to a boil, and simmer until tender, about 30 minutes. Drain and cool. Peel and cut into ¼-inch slices.

To prepare a vinaigrette, whisk together the olive oil, vinegar, shallot, orange juice and zest in a small bowl.

Peel the oranges, and segment them over a bowl to catch the juice, removing all of the white membrane.

Combine the orange segments with the juice, sliced beets, vinaigrette, mint, and feta cheese, and season to taste with salt and pepper.

Fold in the salad greens and divide among 4 plates.

RECOMMENDED WINE
Cuvée Rouge (Sparkling) 2002
V. Sattui Winery • St. Helena, California

ALTERNATIVES
Gamay or *Sparkling Wine*

WARM ARUGULA AND PORTOBELLO SALAD

Serves 2

2 tablespoons olive oil
3 large shallots, sliced
2 large portobello mushrooms, sliced
6 cups baby arugula
½ cup crumbled feta or goat cheese
⅓ cup toasted pine nuts
   Balsamic vinegar
   Sea salt and freshly ground black pepper

Heat the olive oil in a medium sauté pan over medium heat. Add the shallots and mushrooms, and sauté until soft and fragrant.

Put the arugula, feta cheese, and pine nuts in a serving bowl and mix. Top with the hot shallot mixture and toss gently. Add the balsamic vinegar, and salt and pepper to taste.

Serve immediately.

VARIATION Use spinach or dandelion greens instead of the baby arugula.

RECOMMENDED WINE
Santa Cruz Mountain Chardonnay
Thomas Fogarty Winery • Santa Cruz, California

ALTERNATIVES
Chardonnay or *Sauvignon Blanc*

QUINOA AND BLACK BEAN SALAD

Serves 4

Salad

1 cup quinoa

3 cups water

½ teaspoon salt

1 can (15 ounces) black beans, drained and rinsed

2 cups red and/or yellow tomatoes, diced

1 cup finely chopped red bell pepper

2 teaspoons minced green chilies (optional)

2 green onions, minced

¼ cup finely chopped coriander

Sea salt and freshly ground black pepper

Dressing

5 tablespoons fresh lime juice

1 teaspoon salt

1 teaspoon ground cumin

½ teaspoon ground coriander

2 tablespoons red wine vinegar

3 tablespoons olive oil

To prepare the salad: Wash the quinoa and drain it well.

Bring 3 cups of water and ½ teaspoon salt to a boil in a saucepan, then add the quinoa. Lower the heat, cover, and simmer gently until the quinoa is tender, 12 to 15 minutes. Drain and transfer the quinoa to a large bowl and cool.

Add the black beans, tomatoes, bell pepper, chilies, green onions, and coriander, and toss well. Add salt and pepper to taste.

To prepare the dressing: Whisk together the lime juice, salt, cumin, coriander, and vinegar in a small bowl. Add the oil in a stream, whisking.

Drizzle the dressing over the salad and toss well. Season to taste with salt and pepper.

Serve at room temperature.

RECOMMENDED WINE
Pinot Noir Los Carneros
Robert Sinskey Vineyards • Napa, California

ALTERNATIVES
Pinot Noir or *Chardonnay*

TOMATO, WATERMELON, AND FETA SALAD

Serves 4

2 cups diced watermelon
2 cups diced red or yellow tomatoes
½ red onion, thinly sliced
2 tablespoons chopped fresh mint leaves
2 tablespoons chopped fresh basil leaves
2 tablespoons balsamic vinegar
⅓ cup crumbled feta cheese
1 teaspoon peeled and grated fresh ginger
½ teaspoon sea salt
   Freshly ground black pepper

Combine the watermelon, tomatoes, onion, mint, and basil in a salad bowl. Add the vinegar, feta cheese, ginger, salt, and pepper to taste, stirring to combine.

Serve chilled.

RECOMMENDED WINE
2004 Pinot Gris Reserve
Chehalem ◆ Willamette Valley, Oregon

ALTERNATIVES
Sparkling Wine or *Pinot Blanc*

APPLE, WALNUT, AND POMEGRANATE SALAD

Serves 2

3 tablespoons fresh orange juice
1 teaspoon finely minced orange zest
1 teaspoon honey
2 cups chopped apples
½ cup pomegranate seeds
½ cup walnut halves, toasted
¼ cup shaved Romano cheese

In a small bowl, whisk together the orange juice, zest, and honey.

Put the apples in a separate bowl, add the orange juice mixture, and toss to combine. Gently stir in the pomegranate seeds, walnuts, and cheese.

Serve chilled or at room temperature.

RECOMMENDED WINE
Provence California Table Wine
Peju Province Winery • Rutherford, California

ALTERNATIVES
Sauvignon Blanc or *Rosé of Pinot Noir*

FRESH TUNA NIÇOISE

Serves 2

8	ounces fresh yellow fin tuna steak
5	tiny new red potatoes
15 to 20	thin green beans
6 to 8	Niçoise or kalamata olives
1	small tomato, cored and sliced
½	small red pepper, sliced
½	small green pepper, sliced
¼	small red onion, sliced
1	hard-boiled egg, quartered
½	cup Balsamic Vinaigrette Dressing (see recipe on page 85)
	Salt and pepper
2	cups mixed greens

Grill or broil the tuna steak. Allow it to cool; cut it into large chunks and set aside.

Halve or quarter the potatoes, and cook until just tender. Chill.

Briefly blanch the beans. Rinse under cold water and chill.

Arrange the tuna steak, potatoes, beans, olives, tomato, red and green peppers, onion, and egg on a large plate. Drizzle with a small amount of Balsamic Vinaigrette Dressing and season to taste with salt and pepper.

Divide the greens between two plates, and serve the remaining dressing as a side to the salad.

RECOMMENDED WINE
Sauvignon Blanc 2004
Robert Karl Cellars ◆ Spokane, Washington

ALTERNATIVE
Sauvignon Blanc or *Chardonnay*

SPICY SESAME NOODLE SALAD

Serves 4

1 pound soba noodles or whole wheat spaghetti

⅓ cup soy sauce

⅓ cup creamy peanut butter, softened in microwave (10 seconds on high)

3 tablespoons rice wine vinegar

2 tablespoons dark sesame oil

1 teaspoon hot chili paste

2 teaspoons honey

3 cups shredded cabbage and carrot mix

1 cup bean sprouts or pea shoots

1 garlic clove, minced

¼ cup chopped cilantro

5 large scallions, thinly sliced, as garnish

2 tablespoons toasted sesame seeds, as garnish

Cook the pasta to al dente. Drain it immediately in a colander and rinse in cold water to chill. Drain the pasta well.

In the bottom of a large bowl, whisk together the soy sauce, peanut butter, vinegar, sesame oil, chili paste, and honey. Add the noodles, cabbage and carrot mix, bean sprouts, garlic, and cilantro; toss to coat evenly with sauce.

Garnish with scallions and sesame seeds before serving.

Adapted from a recipe by Sean Milton, Seattle, Washington

RECOMMENDED WINE
Napa Valley Gewürztraminer 2003
Stony Hill Vineyard ◆ St. Helena, California

ALTERNATIVES
Gewürztraminer or *Riesling*

NORTHWEST CAESAR SALAD

Serves 4

Dressing

2 anchovies

2 garlic cloves, peeled

3 tablespoons fresh lemon juice

1 tablespoon Worcestershire sauce

2 teaspoons Dijon mustard

1 teaspoon hot sauce

Sea salt

¾ teaspoon freshly ground black pepper

¼ cup extra-virgin olive oil

Salad

8 cups romaine lettuce, torn, washed, and spun dry

8 ounces cooked shrimp

¼ cup freshly grated Parmesan

½ cup whole wheat croutons, plus additional for garnish

Salt and pepper

To prepare the dressing: Put the anchovies, garlic, lemon juice, Worcestershire sauce, mustard, hot sauce, salt to taste, and pepper in a blender, and blend until smooth. With the motor running, add the olive oil slowly in a stream.

To prepare the salad: Put the lettuce, shrimp, Parmesan, and croutons in a salad bowl. Pour ⅓ cup of the dressing over the salad, toss, and season to taste with salt and pepper.

Arrange on a serving dish, and top with additional croutons if desired.

VARIATION Substitute smoked salmon (not lox) for the shrimp.

RECOMMENDED WINE
Napa Valley Chardonnay 2004
Cakebread Cellars • Rutherford, California

ALTERNATIVES
Chardonnay or *Sauvignon Blanc*

CHICKEN DUKKAH SALAD

Serves 4

2   whole chicken breast fillets
1   tablespoon Dukkah (Middle Eastern spice mix)
1   tablespoon extra-virgin olive oil
4   tablespoons plain yogurt
3   tablespoons minced fresh mint
6   cups mixed lettuce leaves
½   cup cherry tomatoes
1   cucumber, peeled and diced
½   cup walnuts or almonds, toasted
1   orange, peeled and segmented

Cut the chicken into thick strips and coat each one thoroughly with the Dukkah. Heat 2 teaspoons of the olive oil in a heavy pan; add the chicken and cook it slowly, until tender. Set the chicken aside to cool slightly.

Mix the yogurt with the mint; refrigerate for 5 to 10 minutes.

Toss the lettuce with the tomatoes, cucumber, nuts, and orange segments. Drizzle the remaining 1 teaspoon of olive oil onto the salad and mix well.

Divide the lettuce mixture among 4 salad plates; top each with an equal amount of the chicken. Pour 1 tablespoon of the yogurt mixture over the chicken and serve.

NOTE   Dukkah can be found in specialty food stores and Middle Eastern markets.

Courtesy of Dr. & Mrs. Justin Ardill, Reilly's Wines, Australia

RECOMMENDED WINE
Old Bushvine Grenache 2004
Reilly's Wines • Mintaro, Clare Valley, South Australia

ALTERNATIVES
Grenache or *Syrah*

ASIAN CHICKEN COLESLAW

Serves 4

3 tablespoons soy sauce
2 tablespoons grated fresh ginger
2 tablespoons rice wine vinegar
2 tablespoons Asian sesame oil
1 tablespoon brown sugar
1 garlic clove, minced
½ teaspoon dried crushed red peppers
4 cups cooked chicken, shredded
1 bag (16 ounces) coleslaw mix
3 stalks celery, thinly sliced
½ bunch green onions, thinly sliced
½ cup chopped cilantro
2 tablespoons toasted sesame seeds
    Salt and pepper

Whisk the soy sauce, ginger, vinegar, sesame oil, brown sugar, garlic, and red peppers in a large bowl to blend.

Mix in the chicken; let it stand for 5 minutes.

Add the coleslaw mix, celery, onions, cilantro, and sesame seeds, stirring to combine. Season to taste with salt and pepper.

Chill for at least 1 hour and up to 3 hours to blend flavors, tossing occasionally.

RECOMMENDED WINE
Riesling Cole Ranch 2004
Handley Cellars • Philo, California

ALTERNATIVES
Riesling or *Gewürztraminer*

STRAWBERRY, SPINACH, AND PECAN SALAD

Serves 4

8 to 10 cups fresh spinach
    3 tablespoons balsamic vinegar
    2 tablespoons rice vinegar
    4 teaspoons honey
    1 tablespoon Dijon mustard
      Sea salt and freshly ground black pepper
    1 pint strawberries, sliced
    2 tablespoons coarsely chopped toasted pecans
   ¼ small red onion, thinly sliced
    1 container (4 ounces) bleu cheese, crumbled

Tear the spinach into bite-size pieces and put into a large bowl.

In a separate bowl, whisk together the vinegars, honey, and mustard; salt and pepper to taste. Add to the spinach and toss to coat.

Add the strawberries, pecans, onion, and bleu cheese. Toss lightly.

RECOMMENDED WINE
Napa Valley Sparkling Rosé 2004
Goosecross Cellars • Yountville, California

ALTERNATIVES
Chardonnay or *Zinfandel*

WILD RICE SALAD
WITH DRIED CHERRIES AND HAZELNUTS
Serves 4

Dressing

¼ cup canola oil

2 tablespoons cider vinegar

1 tablespoon brown sugar

1 teaspoon ground cumin

   Pinch of cardamom

   Sea salt and freshly ground black pepper

Salad

2 cups basmati or jasmine rice, cooked and cooled

2 cups wild rice, cooked and cooled

½ cup dried cherries

½ cup coarsely chopped hazelnuts, toasted

2 tablespoons chopped parsley

To prepare the dressing: Whisk the canola oil, vinegar, brown sugar, cumin, and cardamom together in a small bowl until blended. Season to taste with salt and pepper.

To prepare the salad: Combine the rice, cherries, hazelnuts, and parsley in a large bowl.

Add the dressing to the salad, and toss to combine.

VARIATION Substitute pecans for hazelnuts.

> RECOMMENDED WINE
> *Sauvignon Blanc Napa Valley*
> Work Vineyard ♦ Calistoga, California
>
> ALTERNATIVES
> *Sauvignon Blanc* or *Riesling*

JAPANESE SPINACH SALAD
WITH SESAME DRESSING

Serves 4

1 pound baby spinach, washed

Dressing

2 tablespoons toasted sesame seeds

1 to 2 tablespoons soy sauce

1 to 2 tablespoons rice wine vinegar

1 to 2 tablespoons sesame oil

1 teaspoon raw sugar

To prepare the spinach: Cook the spinach in boiling water until it is barely wilted, 1 to 2 minutes. Drain, then rinse with cold water. Drain well. Squeeze the excess water from the spinach.

To prepare the dressing: Mix the sesame seeds with the soy sauce, rice wine vinegar, sesame oil, and sugar. Start with 1 tablespoon of each ingredient and adjust to your taste.

Toss the spinach with the sesame dressing and chill.

VARIATION Teriyaki sauce can be used instead of soy sauce, but if it is, the sugar should be omitted.

Courtesy of Sean Milton, Seattle, Washington

RECOMMENDED WINE
Gewürztraminer 2004
Corey Creek Vineyards ◆ Cutchogue, New York

ALTERNATIVES
Gewürztraminer or *Riesling*

SHRIMP AND WHITE BEAN SALAD

Serves 4

1 pound small or medium shrimp, shelled and deveined
1 can (19 ounces) cannelloni beans (or other white bean),
     drained and rinsed
1 English cucumber, peeled and diced
1 medium tomato, peeled, seeded, and diced
⅓ cup chopped fresh parsley
⅓ cup diced red onion
⅓ cup diced celery
    Juice and finely minced zest of 1 lemon
2 tablespoons balsamic vinegar
2 tablespoons extra-virgin olive oil
2 garlic cloves, minced
    Sea salt and freshly ground black pepper

Combine the shrimp, beans, cucumber, tomato, parsley, onion, celery,
lemon juice and zest, vinegar, oil, and garlic in a large bowl. Season to
taste with salt and pepper.

RECOMMENDED WINE
Salus Chardonnay 2004
Staglin Family Vineyard ◆ Rutherford, California

ALTERNATIVES
Chardonnay or *Sauvignon Blanc*

WILD GREENS AND SHRIMP
WITH CUCUMBER YOGURT DRESSING

Serves 4

Dressing

1 bell pepper, seeded and chopped
3 green onions, chopped
1 English cucumber, chopped and seeded
1 cup plain yogurt
1 tablespoon canola oil
1 tablespoon fresh lemon juice
1 teaspoon sea salt
   Freshly ground black pepper

Salad

10 cups mixed wild greens
 8 ounces shrimp, cooked and peeled
½ cup chopped parsley

To prepare the dressing: Put the bell pepper, onions, cucumber, yogurt, oil, lemon juice, and salt in a blender and puree until smooth. Chill. Adjust the seasoning of the dressing with salt and pepper prior to serving.

To prepare the salad: Combine the greens, shrimp, and parsley in a salad bowl. Add the dressing and toss lightly.

VARIATION Substitute crabmeat for the shrimp.

Courtesy of Shirlene DeSantis, Sierra Vista, California

RECOMMENDED WINE
Sauvignon Blanc 2003
Silverado Vineyards ◆ Napa, California

ALTERNATIVES
Sauvignon Blanc or *Pinot Blanc*

ROMAINE HEARTS
WITH GORGONZOLA-WALNUT VINAIGRETTE
Serves 4

Dressing
- ½ cup extra-virgin olive oil
- ⅓ cup crumbled Gorgonzola cheese
- ¼ cup sherry vinegar
- ¼ cup walnuts, toasted
- 2 garlic cloves, peeled
- 1 tablespoon spicy brown mustard
- 1 teaspoon honey
  Sea salt and freshly ground black pepper

Salad
- 2 bunches romaine hearts, washed, trimmed, and dried
- 1 ripe tomato, seeded and thinly sliced
- 1 avocado, peeled and sliced
- 2 green onions, thinly sliced

To prepare the dressing: Put the oil, Gorgonzola, vinegar, walnuts, garlic, mustard, and honey in a blender and blend until smooth. Add salt and pepper to taste. Chill until ready to serve.

To prepare the salad: Tear the romaine into bite-size pieces and transfer it to a salad bowl along with the tomato, avocado, and green onions. Add the dressing, tossing to combine.

RECOMMENDED WINE
Roero Arneis
Bruno Giacosa ◆ Piedmont, Italy

ALTERNATIVES
Arneis or *Pinot Gris*

WARM ASIAN CHICKEN SALAD

Serves 4

1 pound boneless chicken breast, cut in ¼-inch strips
2 tablespoons cornstarch
1 teaspoon hot chili oil
2 teaspoons sesame oil
1 small red onion, thinly sliced
1 cup snow pea pods
½ red bell pepper, seeded and thinly sliced
4 large shiitake mushrooms, thinly sliced
2 tablespoons rice wine vinegar
2 tablespoons soy sauce
¼ cup low-sodium chicken or vegetable broth
1 teaspoon salt
¼ teaspoon freshly ground black pepper
8 cups spinach or mixed greens
¼ cup toasted sesame seeds, as garnish

Toss the chicken with the cornstarch; toss again with the hot chili oil.

Heat the sesame oil in a large nonstick sauté pan over medium-high heat. Sauté the chicken until golden brown, 3 to 4 minutes. Remove the chicken from the pan and set aside. Combine the onion, pea pods, bell pepper, and mushrooms in the same pan; cook for 2 minutes. Add the vinegar, soy sauce, broth, salt, and pepper; cook until the liquid boils, about 1 minute.

Divide the salad greens among 4 plates. Top with the chicken mixture and garnish with sesame seeds.

RECOMMENDED WINE
Sauvignon Blanc (Juliana Vineyards) 2004
Merryvale Vineyards • St. Helena, California

ALTERNATIVES
Sauvignon Blanc or *Riesling*

CHICKPEA ARTICHOKE SALAD

Serves 4

1 jar (6 ounces) marinated artichoke hearts, drained and
    quartered (reserve marinade)
1 can (15 ounces) chickpeas, drained and rinsed
2 tablespoons chopped parsley
¼ cup toasted pine nuts
¼ cup grated Parmesan
    Juice and zest of 1 lemon
2 tablespoons balsamic vinegar
1 tablespoon extra-virgin olive oil
1 teaspoon Dijon mustard
1 garlic clove, minced
1 tablespoon chopped fresh oregano, or 1 teaspoon dried

In a large bowl, combine the artichoke hearts, chickpeas, parsley, pine nuts, and Parmesan.

Whisk together the reserved artichoke marinade, lemon juice and zest, vinegar, olive oil, Dijon mustard, garlic, and oregano. Add to the artichoke mixture, tossing to combine.

NOTE Serve on a bed of arugula, if desired.

RECOMMENDED WINE
Sauvignon Blanc Russian River Valley 2004
Hanna Winery • Healdsburg, California

ALTERNATIVES
Sauvignon Blanc or *Chardonnay*

MEDITERRANEAN LENTIL SALAD

Serves 6

2 cups lentils
4 cups water
6 cloves
1 carrot, peeled and halved
1 garlic clove
1 bay leaf
1 teaspoon dried oregano
1 teaspoon salt
¼ cup balsamic vinegar
¼ cup extra-virgin olive oil
2 cups cherry tomatoes, halved
½ cup slivered almonds, blanched and toasted
½ cup chopped parsley
½ cup crumbled feta cheese
⅓ cup thinly sliced green onions
  Salt and pepper

Combine the lentils and water in a large saucepan over medium-high heat. Stick 3 cloves into each carrot half and add them to the lentils. Stir in the garlic, bay leaf, oregano, and salt. Cover and bring to a boil; simmer until the lentils are tender, about 15 minutes. Drain; discard the carrot, garlic, and bay leaf.

Whisk together the balsamic vinegar and olive oil.

Put the lentils into a large bowl and toss with the vinegar and oil. Cool.

Combine the lentils with the tomatoes, almonds, parsley, feta cheese, and green onions; season to taste with salt and pepper.

Cover and chill until ready to serve.

Courtesy of Lynn Baker, Sisters, Oregon

RECOMMENDED WINE
Vallée de la Lune 2002
Kunde Estate Winery and Vineyards
Kenwood, California

ALTERNATIVES
Grenache or *Mourvèdre*

GRILLED CORN, PAPAYA,
AND BLACK BEAN SALAD
WITH TOASTED CUMIN SEED DRESSING

Serves 6

⅓ cup pineapple juice
2 tablespoons olive oil
   Juice and finely chopped zest of 1 lime
2 tablespoons cumin seeds, toasted
1 teaspoon granulated sugar
2 medium ripe papayas, peeled, seeded, and chopped
3 medium ears of grilled corn, kernels cut from the cob
1 red bell pepper, diced
1 can (15 ounces) black beans, drained and rinsed
¼ cup chopped cilantro
¼ cup chopped red onion
¼ teaspoon salt

In a large bowl, stir together the pineapple juice, olive oil, lime juice and zest, cumin seeds, and sugar.

Stir in the papaya, coating it well with the dressing. Add the corn, bell pepper, beans, cilantro, onion, and salt, stirring well to combine.

Serve chilled or at room temperature.

RECOMMENDED WINE
Arneis 2004
Ponzi Vineyards ◆ Beaverton, Oregon

ALTERNATIVES
Arneis or *Pinot Blanc*

CRAB, MANGO, AND GINGER SALAD
Serves 4

1 pound crabmeat
1 English cucumber, peeled, seeded, and thinly sliced
1 large ripe mango, peeled and diced
¼ cup chopped fresh mint
   Juice and finely chopped zest of 1 lime
3 tablespoons extra-virgin olive oil
1 tablespoon grated fresh ginger
1 red chili, stemmed, seeded, and finely chopped
   Sea salt and freshly ground black pepper
   Arugula, frisée, or other salad greens

In a large bowl, combine the crabmeat, cucumber, mango, and fresh mint.

In a small bowl, whisk together the lime juice and zest, olive oil, ginger, and red chili. Add to the crabmeat mixture, and season to taste with salt and pepper.

Put salad greens on 4 plates and top with the crab mixture.

RECOMMENDED WINE
Blanc de Noirs NV
Domaine Chandon • Yountville, California

ALTERNATIVES
Sparkling White Wine or Riesling

STRAWBERRY CHICKEN SALAD

Serves 4

- ¾ cup 100% canola mayonnaise
- ¼ cup chopped chutney
- 1 tablespoon fresh lemon juice
- 1 teaspoon grated lemon zest
- 1 tablespoon good quality curry powder
- 1 garlic clove, minced
- ¼ teaspoon chopped fresh ginger
- 1 teaspoon salt
- 3 cups diced cooked chicken
- 1 cup sliced celery
- 2 green onions, sliced
- ½ cup chopped red bell pepper
- 2 cups sliced fresh strawberries
- 2 tablespoons chopped fresh basil
- Lettuce leaves
- 1 cup whole fresh strawberries, as garnish

In a large bowl, mix together the mayonnaise, chutney, lemon juice, lemon zest, curry powder, garlic, ginger, and salt. Add the chicken, celery, onion, and bell pepper; toss to combine. Cover and chill.

Just before serving, gently toss the sliced strawberries and basil with the chicken mixture.

Line a platter or individual plates with lettuce leaves. Mound the chicken mixture on top of the lettuce and garnish with whole strawberries.

RECOMMENDED WINE
Gamay Rouge 2004
V. Sattui Winery • St. Helena, California

ALTERNATIVE
Gamay or *Sauvignon Blanc*

CURRIED SPINACH SALAD

Serves 6

Dressing

⅓ cup red wine vinegar
½ cup canola oil
1 teaspoon dry mustard
1 tablespoon Major Grey chutney
1 teaspoon good quality curry powder
1 teaspoon salt
3 drops of Tabasco

Salad

1 large bunch spinach, washed and stemmed
1 tart red apple, chopped
¾ cup golden raisins
4 green onions, chopped
⅔ cup chopped peanuts or walnuts (salted optional)
2 tablespoons toasted sesame seeds

To prepare the dressing: Combine all the ingredients in a jar and shake well. Let the dressing stand at room temperature for two hours. Adjust seasoning to taste.

To prepare the salad: Tear the spinach into bite-size pieces and put them in a large salad bowl. Add the apple, raisins, onions, nuts, and sesame seeds.

Dress lightly, using half of the prepared dressing and reserving the rest.

Courtesy of Anne Lagen, Bellevue, Washington

RECOMMENDED WINE
Riesling Columbia Valley 2005
Seven Hills Winery • Walla Walla, Washington

ALTERNATIVES
Riesling or *Gewürztraminer*

POMEGRANATE VINAIGRETTE

Makes ½ cup

- ¼ cup pomegranate juice (fresh or bottled)
- 1 teaspoon Dijon mustard
- 3 tablespoons light olive oil

Combine all the ingredients in a jar and shake well.

NOTES To serve, drizzle over your favorite greens. This vinaigrette is especially good with full-bodied greens like spinach or arugula. The dressing will keep for 1 week, covered and chilled.

DIJON BALSAMIC VINAIGRETTE

Makes ¾ cup

- ½ cup extra-virgin olive oil
- ⅛ cup balsamic vinegar
- 1 heaping teaspoon Dijon mustard
- 1 heaping teaspoon 100% canola mayonnaise
- ¼ teaspoon dry herbes de Provence (optional)

In a small bowl, whisk the olive oil, vinegar, mustard, and mayonnaise together until smooth and creamy.

If using the dried herbes de Provence, crush to a powder and add to the dressing, whisking to combine.

NOTE Serve over salad greens.

ELEVEN

SOUPS

ITALIAN VEGETABLE SOUP

Serves 4 to 6

1 tablespoon olive oil
2 leeks, finely chopped
2 medium carrots, peeled and finely chopped
2 garlic cloves, minced
1 large zucchini, coarsely chopped
1 can (15 ounces) white beans, drained
1 can (14 ounces) water-packed artichoke hearts, drained and
     quartered
1 can (14½ ounces) tomatoes, diced
3 cups low-sodium chicken or vegetable broth
1 tablespoon chopped fresh thyme leaves
1 bunch spinach or Swiss chard greens, washed and coarsely chopped
   Sea salt and freshly ground black pepper
   Freshly grated Parmesan

Heat the olive oil in a large nonstick soup pot over medium heat. Add the leeks, carrots, and garlic, and sauté until tender. Stir in the zucchini and sauté for 2 minutes.

Add the beans, artichoke, tomatoes, broth, and thyme, and bring to a simmer. Cover and simmer gently until the flavor develops, stirring occasionally, about 20 minutes.

Stir in the greens, and season to taste with salt and pepper. Cook for 2 minutes.

Place one third of the soup into a food processor or blender and puree until thick. Return to the soup pot and mix well. Season to taste with salt and pepper.

Ladle the soup into bowls and sprinkle with Parmesan cheese.

RECOMMENDED WINE
Langhe Nebbiolo 2002
Aurelio Settimo ◆ La Morra, Italy

ALTERNATIVES
Nebbiolo or *Sangiovese*

SHRIMP GAZPACHO

Serves 4 to 6

12 ounces shrimp, cooked, shelled, and deveined
 4 large ripe tomatoes, peeled, seeded, and finely chopped
 1 stalk celery, finely chopped
 1 small red bell pepper, finely chopped
 1 small green bell pepper, finely chopped
 1 medium cucumber, peeled, seeded, and finely chopped
 ½ sweet onion, finely chopped
 ½ large jalapeño chili, seeded and finely chopped
1½ cups tomato juice
 ½ cup bottled clam juice
 ¼ cup chopped cilantro
 3 tablespoons balsamic vinegar
 2 garlic cloves, minced
 1 tablespoon fresh lemon juice
 1 tablespoon extra-virgin olive oil
 ½ teaspoon ground cumin
   Sea salt and freshly ground black pepper
   Tabasco
   Fat-free sour cream, as garnish

Chop the shrimp into bite-size pieces.

In a large bowl, combine the tomatoes, celery, bell peppers, cucumber, onion, jalapeño, tomato juice, clam juice, cilantro, vinegar, garlic, lemon juice, oil, and cumin. Gently fold the shrimp into the tomato mixture. Season to taste with salt, pepper, and Tabasco.

Cover and chill for at least 3 hours and up to 24 hours to allow the flavors to blend.

To serve, ladle the soup into serving bowls and garnish with a spoonful of sour cream.

RECOMMENDED WINE
Roussanne Napa Valley 2003
Truchard Vineyards • Carneros, California

ALTERNATIVES
Meursault or *Pinot Gris*

CHICKEN DIABLO SOUP

Serves 4

1 tablespoon olive oil
1 cup diced yellow onion
½ cup diced green pepper
½ cup diced zucchini
½ cup diced celery
1 teaspoon chopped garlic
8 ounces cooked chicken breast, chopped
2 medium tomatoes, seeded and diced
6 cups vegetable stock
¼ cup sliced kalamata olives
½ teaspoon oregano
½ teaspoon chili powder
¼ teaspoon cayenne
Sea salt and freshly ground black pepper

Heat the olive oil in a nonstick soup pot over medium-high heat. Add the onion, green pepper, zucchini, celery, and garlic, and sauté until it starts to brown.

Add the chicken, tomatoes, vegetable stock, olives, oregano, chili powder, and cayenne. Bring to a simmer and cook for 15 minutes. Season to taste with salt and pepper.

Courtesy of Ghini's French Caffe, Tucson, Arizona

RECOMMENDED WINE
Mazzocco Carignane 1999
Mazzocco Vineyards • Healdsburg, California

ALTERNATIVES
Zinfandel or *Grenache*

WILD MUSHROOM AND BARLEY SOUP

Serves 4

1 tablespoon extra-virgin olive oil
1 cup chopped onion
3 garlic cloves, minced
1 pound assorted wild mushrooms (shiitake, oyster, Portobello), sliced
4 cups low-sodium chicken broth
2 tablespoons sherry (optional)
1 tablespoon chopped fresh thyme or ½ teaspoon dried
1½ cups barley, cooked
  Sea salt and freshly ground black pepper
½ cup plain yogurt, as garnish

In a large sauté pan, heat the olive oil over medium heat. Add the onion and garlic, and sauté for 5 minutes. Add the mushrooms, chicken broth, and sherry, if using. If using dried thyme, add it at this point. Bring to a simmer, cover, and cook for 20 minutes.

Puree about half of the soup in a blender, then return it to the pan. Add the cooked barley and fresh thyme, if using, and season to taste with salt and pepper. Heat until warm.

To serve, ladle into serving bowls and garnish with a spoonful of plain yogurt.

RECOMMENDED WINE
La Famiglia Barbera
La Famiglia di Robert Mondavi Winery
Healdsburg, California

ALTERNATIVES
Barbera or *Sangiovese*

MISO SOUP WITH GARLIC AND GINGER

Serves 4

2	teaspoons sesame oil
4	shiitake mushrooms, sliced
1	small carrot, peeled and grated
2	green onions, thinly sliced
½	cup shredded Napa cabbage
2	teaspoons minced ginger
1	garlic clove, minced
4	cups vegetable stock
2	teaspoons soy sauce
1	8-ounce package silken tofu, cubed
3 to 4	tablespoons miso paste
	Toasted sesame seeds, as garnish

Heat the oil in a medium nonstick saucepan over medium-high heat. Add the mushrooms, carrot, onion, cabbage, ginger, and garlic, and sauté for about 2 minutes.

Add the stock, soy sauce, and tofu, and bring to a boil. Simmer for 2 minutes.

Dissolve the miso in ½ cup of the hot broth. Add it back to the soup and cook for another 2 minutes. Be sure not to boil the soup once you have added the miso.

Ladle the soup into bowls and garnish with toasted sesame seeds.

NOTE Try miso soup for breakfast.

VARIATIONS Experiment with other soup additions: bok choy, leeks, okra, squash, potatoes, snow pea pods, green beans, daikon radish, bean sprouts, wakame seaweed, or shrimp.

RECOMMENDED WINE
Casa Nuestra Dry Chenin Blanc 2005
Casa Nuestra Winery ♦ St. Helena, California

ALTERNATIVES
Chenin Blanc or *Gewürztraminer*

TORTELLINI, SPINACH, AND TOMATO SOUP

Serves 4

1   tablespoon olive oil
5   garlic cloves, minced
½   cup chopped onion
5   cups low-sodium chicken or vegetable broth
2   teaspoons Italian seasoning
1   teaspoon salt
9   ounces cheese tortellini, fresh or frozen
1   can (14½ ounces) diced tomatoes, with liquid
1   pound spinach, stemmed and coarsely chopped
¾   cup coarsely chopped fresh basil leaves
1   cup grated Parmesan
    Sea salt and black pepper

In a large saucepan, heat the olive oil over medium heat. Add the garlic and onion, and sauté for 2 to 3 minutes.

Add the broth, Italian seasoning, and salt, and bring to a boil. Add the tortellini and cook about 5 minutes if using frozen pasta, less if using fresh pasta. Stir in the tomatoes; cook just until the pasta is tender, about 3 minutes.

Stir in the spinach, basil, and ¾ cup of the Parmesan; cook until wilted, about 1 minute. Season to taste with salt and pepper.

Ladle into bowls and garnish with the remaining Parmesan.

> RECOMMENDED WINE
> *Goldeneye Anderson Valley Pinot Noir 2002*
> Goldeneye Winery • Anderson Valley, California
>
> ALTERNATIVES
> *Pinot Noir* or *Grenache*

GINGERED BUTTERNUT SQUASH AND APPLE SOUP

Serves 6

1 tablespoon canola oil
1 medium onion, chopped
2½ pounds butternut squash, peeled, seeded, and cubed
2 small Gala apples, peeled, cored, and chopped
1 tablespoon grated ginger
5 cups low-sodium chicken broth
1 cup apple juice or apple cider
½ teaspoon ground ginger
½ teaspoon nutmeg
Sea salt and freshly ground black pepper
Plain yogurt, as garnish

Heat the oil in a large nonstick soup pot over medium heat. Sauté the onion until soft, about 3 minutes.

Stir in the squash, apples, and ginger; cook for 2 minutes. Add the broth, apple juice, ginger, and nutmeg. Bring to a boil, cover, and simmer about 20 minutes, or until the squash is tender. Season to taste with salt and pepper. Cool slightly.

Working in batches, puree the soup in a blender.

Ladle into 6 bowls and serve with a spoonful of yogurt as garnish.

RECOMMENDED WINE
2004 Riesling—Los Carneros
Robert Sinskey Vineyards • Napa, California

ALTERNATIVES
Riesling or *Gewürztraminer*

VIETNAMESE NOODLE SOUP

Serves 4 to 6

¾ pound beef sirloin
8 cups beef broth
1 slice ginger, 2 inches thick
2 whole star anise
1 cinnamon stick
12 ounces rice vermicelli noodles
¼ cup Asian fish sauce
3 tablespoons fresh lime juice
   Sea salt and freshly ground black pepper
2 cups fresh bean sprouts, rinsed and drained
4 green onions, thinly sliced
⅓ cup fresh cilantro leaves
⅓ cup fresh mint leaves
⅓ cup fresh basil leaves
2 small red chilies, thinly sliced
   Hot chili sauce
   Hoisin sauce
   Lime wedges, as garnish

Freeze beef for 1 hour.

In a 2-quart saucepan, bring the broth, ginger, star anise, and cinnamon to a boil. Reduce heat and simmer for 15 minutes. Remove from heat and set aside.

With a very sharp knife, cut the sirloin across the grain into very thin slices.

In a large bowl, soak the noodles in hot water to cover until they are softened and pliable, about 15 minutes. While the noodles are soaking, bring a kettle of salted water to a boil.

Drain the noodles in a colander, then put them into the boiling water, stirring, and cook until tender, about 45 seconds. Drain the noodles in a colander. Set aside.

Strain the broth into a saucepan and bring it to a boil. Stir in the fish sauce and lime juice, and add salt and pepper to taste.

Add the sirloin and cook until the sirloin changes color, about 30 to 45 seconds. Skim any froth from the soup.

To serve, divide the noodles into 4 large bowls; top with bean sprouts. Ladle the soup over the noodles. Sprinkle the soup with the green onions, cilantro, mint, basil, and chilies. Season to taste with chili sauce and hoisin sauce, and serve with lime wedges as garnish.

RECOMMENDED WINE
Gewürztraminer 2004
Lazy Creek Vineyards • Mendocino, California

ALTERNATIVES
Gewürztraminer or *Riesling*

ASIAN WATERMELON-CUCUMBER SOUP WITH CRAB

Serves 4

Soup

- 5 cups coarsely chopped watermelon (from a 4-pound piece, rind discarded), seeded
- 2 cups peeled, seeded, and coarsely chopped English cucumber
- 1 tablespoon olive oil
- 1 lemongrass stalk, minced
- 2 tablespoons peeled and finely chopped fresh ginger
- 2 tablespoons finely chopped green onion
- 1 tablespoon finely chopped garlic
- 1 small hot green chili (such as Thai or serrano), finely chopped
  Juice of 1 lime
  Sea salt
- ⅓ cup plain yogurt

Crab

- 12 ounces (about 2 cups) jumbo lump crabmeat (preferably Dungeness), picked over
- ½ cup seeded and diced red tomato
- ¼ cup finely chopped fresh cilantro
  Lime wedges, as garnish

To prepare the soup: Puree the watermelon and cucumber in a blender or food processor until smooth, and transfer to a bowl.

Heat the oil in a 2-quart heavy saucepan over moderately low heat. Add the lemongrass, ginger, green onion, and garlic; cook, stirring, about 5 minutes. Add 1 cup of the watermelon puree and simmer, stirring, for an additional 5 minutes.

Remove the watermelon mixture from the heat, and transfer it to the blender along with the chili and lime juice; blend until smooth. Add the remaining watermelon puree and blend briefly.

Season to taste with additional chili, lime juice, and salt if desired, blending if necessary. Pour the soup through a sieve into a bowl. Stir in the yogurt and season to taste with salt. Chill.

To prepare the crab: Gently combine the crabmeat with the tomato and cilantro.

Divide the crab mixture among 4 soup plates, mounding in the center. Pour the chilled soup around the crab.

Serve with lime wedges as garnish.

RECOMMENDED WINE
Anderson Valley Gewürztraminer 2004
Handley Cellars • Philo, California

ALTERNATIVES
Gewürztraminer or *Riesling*

CURRIED RED LENTIL SOUP WITH LIME

Serves 4 to 6

1 tablespoon extra-virgin olive oil
1 large onion, chopped
3 garlic cloves, minced
1 tablespoon minced ginger
1 tablespoon Madras curry powder
1 teaspoon cumin
⅛ teaspoon cayenne pepper
1 cup red lentils, rinsed and sorted
5 cups low-sodium chicken or vegetable broth
  Sea salt and freshly ground black pepper
1 bag (6 ounces) of baby spinach
  Juice and zest of 1 lime
  Plain yogurt, as garnish
  Chopped fresh mint, as garnish

In a large saucepan, heat the oil over medium-high heat. Add the onion, garlic, and ginger, and sauté until the onion is tender, 4 to 5 minutes. Stir in the curry powder, cumin, and cayenne, and stir-fry for 30 seconds.

Add the lentils and broth, cover, and bring to a boil over high heat. Reduce heat to medium-low and simmer, stirring occasionally, until the lentils are tender, about 30 to 40 minutes. Season to taste with salt and pepper.

Add the spinach and lime juice with zest just before serving. Garnish with a spoonful of yogurt and the chopped mint.

RECOMMENDED WINE
Lamborn "Papa's Vintage" Zinfandel 2003
Lamborn Family Vineyards • Orinda, California

ALTERNATIVES
Zinfandel or *Syrah*

VEGETABLES AND SIDE DISHES

PAN-ROASTED ORANGE CARROTS
Serves 4

1 tablespoon olive oil
1 pound small carrots, peeled, and cut in half if desired
2 oranges, peeled and segmented
4 garlic cloves, minced
¼ cup white wine
1 tablespoon chopped thyme
1 tablespoon chopped rosemary
1 teaspoon minced orange zest
   Sea salt and freshly ground black pepper

Preheat oven to 425°F.

Heat the oil in a large ovenproof nonstick sauté pan over medium heat. Add the carrots, orange segments, and garlic, and cook over low heat for 3 to 4 minutes, turning frequently.

Add the wine, thyme, rosemary, and orange zest; season to taste with salt and pepper.

Place the sauté pan in the oven, and cook until tender, about 10 to 15 minutes.

WILD MUSHROOM–HAZELNUT MEDLEY

Serves 4

2 tablespoons sherry
1 tablespoon sesame oil
1 teaspoon Chinese five-spice powder
½ teaspoon sea salt
1½ pounds wild mushrooms (shiitake, Portobello, cremini, oyster), trimmed and thickly sliced
½ cup coarsely chopped hazelnuts, toasted
¼ cup chopped Italian parsley
Freshly ground black pepper

Preheat oven to 450°F.

In a large bowl, combine the sherry, sesame oil, five-spice powder, and salt. Add the mushrooms and mix well.

Place the mushroom mixture in a nonstick roasting pan in a single layer.

Roast for 8 minutes. Stir in the hazelnuts, and roast until just tender, another 3 to 5 minutes. Stir in the parsley; adjust seasoning with salt and pepper.

Serve hot.

CURRIED CAULIFLOWER PUREE

Serves 4

      1 head of cauliflower (1 to 1½ pounds), trimmed
      1 tablespoon canola oil
      1 small onion, peeled and sliced
      2 garlic cloves, crushed
1 to 1½ cups low-sodium chicken or vegetable broth
      1 tablespoon Madras curry powder
      ⅓ cup plain yogurt
         Sea salt and freshly ground black pepper

Break the cauliflower into florets and chop coarsely.

Heat the oil in a medium saucepan. Add the onion and garlic, and cook until translucent, about 2 minutes.

Add the cauliflower and enough broth to cover; bring to a boil. Cover, reduce heat, and simmer until tender, about 10 minutes.

Drain the cauliflower, reserving ½ cup of the cooking broth, and place the cauliflower in a food processor. Add 1 to 2 tablespoons of the cooking broth, curry powder, and yogurt. Add salt and pepper to taste. Process to the desired consistency. Add more cooking broth if desired. Adjust seasoning to taste.

Serve immediately or transfer the puree to a gratin dish and reheat when ready to serve.

VARIATIONS Omit curry powder and add grated ginger and candied ginger slices, or add a handful of arugula, some Parmesan cheese, and a bit of horseradish.

SPICED SPINACH WITH YOGURT

Serves 2

1 teaspoon extra-virgin olive oil
2 garlic cloves, crushed
2 teaspoons grated ginger
1 teaspoon ground coriander
1 teaspoon ground cumin
1 pound spinach, washed and trimmed
½ cup whole milk yogurt
⅛ teaspoon nutmeg
  Sea salt and freshly ground black pepper
2 tablespoons chopped walnuts or toasted pine nuts

Heat the oil in a large nonstick saucepan over medium-high heat. Add the garlic and ginger, and cook for 1 minute. Stir in the coriander and cumin.

Add the spinach and cook until just wilted, about 2 to 3 minutes. Remove from heat.

Stir in the yogurt and nutmeg; season to taste with salt and pepper.

Top with nuts prior to serving.

ZUCCHINI-MINT SAUTÉ

Serves 2 to 4

1 pound young zucchini, trimmed and cut into ½-inch slices
½ teaspoon salt
1 teaspoon extra-virgin olive oil
2 garlic cloves, minced
2 tablespoons chopped fresh mint
  Sea salt and freshly ground black pepper

In a medium bowl, combine the zucchini and salt. Transfer it to a colander placed over a bowl; allow it to drain for 15 minutes. With a large spoon, press the zucchini lightly to try to remove as much moisture as possible.

In a large nonstick sauté pan, heat the oil over high heat until hot but not smoking. Add the garlic and cook for 1 minute. Add the zucchini and cook, tossing constantly until golden, about 2 minutes. Remove from heat.

Stir in the mint, and season to taste with salt and pepper.

FRESH CORN POLENTA

Serves 4

2 small tomatoes, cored and coarsely chopped
1 tablespoon chopped fresh basil
1½ cups water
1 cup low-fat milk
1 tablespoon canola margarine
1 teaspoon kosher salt
½ cup polenta
1 cup corn kernels, cooked
¼ cup chopped fresh mixed herbs (thyme, rosemary, basil, parsley)
¼ cup freshly grated Parmesan cheese
Kosher salt and freshly ground black pepper

In a small bowl, toss the tomatoes with the basil and set aside.

In a medium-heavy saucepan, combine the water and milk over medium-high heat. Bring to a boil. Add the margarine and salt.

Whisking constantly, add the polenta in a slow, steady stream. Continue to whisk until all lumps have disappeared. Reduce heat to low and simmer gently, stirring constantly with a wooden spoon until the polenta is thick and creamy, about 20 minutes.

Fold in the corn, herbs, and Parmesan cheese; season to taste with salt and pepper.

Spoon into heated bowls and top with the tomato mixture. Serve immediately.

VARIATION Substitute fresh oregano for the fresh basil.

ASIAN RICE PILAF

Serves 4 to 6

Rice

- 1½ cups long grain white rice
- 1 tablespoon canola oil
- 3 garlic cloves, minced
- 1 cup dried currants or raisins
- 4 green onions, minced
- 1 red bell pepper, seeded and minced
- ¼ cup minced cilantro
- ¼ cup toasted pine nuts

Sauce

- 1 cup low-sodium chicken stock
- 1 to 1½ cups dry white wine
- 2 tablespoons soy sauce
- 1 tablespoon Asian sesame oil
- 1 teaspoon Chinese chili sauce
- ½ teaspoon salt
- 1 tablespoon grated tangerine or orange zest

Wash the rice in a sieve under cold water, stirring with your fingers, until the water is no longer cloudy. Drain thoroughly.

To prepare the sauce: Combine all the sauce ingredients in a small bowl and set aside.

To prepare the rice: In a 3-quart saucepan over medium-high heat, combine the oil and garlic; sauté until the mixture sizzles. Add the rice and stir until heated, about 5 minutes.

Add the currants and the prepared sauce and bring it to a low boil, stirring. Cover, reduce heat to lowest setting, and simmer until all liquid is absorbed, about 18 to 24 minutes.

Remove cover and stir in the green onions, bell pepper, cilantro, and pine nuts.

Serve at once.

CUBAN-STYLE BLACK BEANS

Serves 4

1 tablespoon olive oil
½ green bell pepper, finely chopped
1 small onion, finely chopped
4 garlic cloves, minced
2 teaspoons ground cumin
2 teaspoons dried oregano
1 bay leaf
2 cans (15 ounces each) black beans, rinsed and drained
¼ cup dry white wine
1 cup low-sodium chicken or vegetable broth, plus additional
    for thinning the soup if needed
½ teaspoon sugar (optional)
2 tablespoons chopped fresh cilantro
   Salt and freshly ground black pepper

Heat the oil in a large nonstick sauté pan over medium heat. Add the bell pepper, onion, garlic, cumin, oregano, and bay leaf. Cook until the vegetables are soft but not brown, about 5 minutes.

Stir in the black beans and wine, and bring to a boil.

Stir in the broth and sugar, if using. Reduce heat to medium and simmer for 5 minutes. Remove the bay leaf and discard it.

Puree one quarter of the bean mixture in a blender (or mash with the back of a spoon).

Stir the puree back into the simmering beans; add the cilantro. Simmer until thick but still soupy, about 2 minutes more.

If the bean mixture is too thick, add more broth. Season to taste with salt and pepper.

ORZO WITH BROCCOLI RABE AND FETA

Serves 4 to 6

1½ cups orzo
 2 teaspoons olive oil
 2 tablespoons minced garlic
 ½ teaspoon hot chili flakes
 1 pound broccoli rabe, trimmed and coarsely chopped
 1 cup crumbled feta cheese
 ⅔ cup chopped pitted kalamata olives
 ¼ cup chopped and packed fresh basil
 ¼ cup toasted pine nuts
   Sea salt and freshly ground black pepper

In a large pot of boiling salted water, cook the orzo until al dente. Drain, reserving 1 cup of the cooking water, and transfer the orzo to a large bowl.

Meanwhile, heat the oil in a large nonstick sauté pan over medium heat. Add the garlic and stir until fragrant but not brown, 1 to 2 minutes.

Add the chili flakes and broccoli rabe; stir-fry 3 to 4 minutes.

Add ½ cup of the reserved orzo cooking water; simmer until the broccoli rabe is just tender to bite, about 5 to 6 minutes.

Add the broccoli rabe mixture to the orzo along with the feta cheese, olives, basil, and pine nuts, mixing well. If desired, add additional pasta water. Season to taste with salt and pepper.

VARIATION Substitute broccoli florets for the broccoli rabe.

SAUTÉED GREENS AND CANNELLINI BEANS

Serves 4

2 teaspoons olive oil
1 small yellow onion, diced
2 garlic cloves, minced
1 can (15 ounces) cannellini beans, rinsed and drained
12 ounces baby spinach or other greens
   Juice of 1 lemon
¼ teaspoon red pepper flakes
1 tablespoon chopped fresh thyme
   Salt and freshly ground black pepper

Heat the oil in a large nonstick sauté pan over medium heat.

Add the onion and cook until translucent, about 2 minutes; add the garlic and cook for 1 minute. Add the beans and cook until they are hot and slightly softened, about 3 minutes.

Add the spinach, lemon juice, and red pepper flakes, stirring frequently, until the spinach is wilted, about 3 minutes.

Add the thyme, and season to taste with salt and pepper.

SWISS CHARD AND BEAN RISOTTO

Serves 4

3½ cups low-sodium chicken or vegetable both
 1 can (15 ounces) diced Italian tomatoes
 1 tablespoon olive oil
 4 garlic cloves, minced
 1 small onion, minced
1½ cups Arborio rice
 ½ cup dry white wine
 1 can (15 ounces) cannellini beans, rinsed and drained
 2 tablespoons chopped fresh thyme
 1 bunch Swiss chard (1 pound), trimmed and chopped
 1 cup grated pecorino Romano or Parmesan cheese
   Sea salt and freshly ground black pepper
   Lemon wedges (optional)

In a medium saucepan, bring the broth and tomatoes to a boil; reduce heat to maintain a gentle simmer.

Meanwhile, heat the oil in a large heavy saucepan over medium-high heat, add the garlic and onion, and cook until softened, about 5 minutes.

Add the rice, and stir until the grains are well coated with oil. Add the wine and simmer briskly until it is absorbed.

With a ladle, add the hot broth and tomatoes one cup at a time, stirring often. After each addition, let the rice absorb most of the broth before adding more. Add the beans and thyme with the last cup of broth.

Add the chard and stir until the chard begins to wilt, about 3 minutes.

When most of the broth is absorbed and the rice is tender but still al dente, stir in the cheese; season with salt and pepper.

Serve hot, with lemon wedges if you wish.

GINGER-SESAME ASPARAGUS SAUTÉ

Serves 4

1   tablespoon sesame oil
1   garlic clove, chopped
1   tablespoon grated ginger
1   pound asparagus, trimmed and cut on the diagonal into
      2-inch pieces
2   tablespoons hoisin sauce
     Salt and pepper
2   tablespoons toasted sesame seeds

Heat the oil in a large nonstick skillet. Add the garlic and ginger, and stir-fry for 15 seconds.

Add the asparagus and stir-fry until crisp tender, about 4 minutes. Add the hoisin sauce and toss until the asparagus is coated, about 1 minute longer.

Season with salt and pepper, toss with sesame seeds, and serve.

GREEN BEANS WITH PESTO

Serves 4

1	pound green beans, trimmed
2 to 3	tablespoons good quality balsamic vinegar
¼	teaspoon brown sugar
½	cup pesto
	Sea salt and freshly ground black pepper
	Shaved Parmesan or pecorino Romano cheese, as garnish

Steam the green beans until crisp tender, about 4 minutes. Drain well and transfer to a large bowl.

Meanwhile, mix the balsamic vinegar with the brown sugar. Add the pesto and the vinegar mixture to the beans, tossing to combine. Season to taste with salt and pepper.

Add the cheese as garnish, and serve at once.

QUINOA PILAF

Serves 4

1 tablespoon olive oil
1 small onion, finely chopped
½ red bell pepper, finely chopped
½ yellow bell pepper, finely chopped
½ cup finely chopped carrot
2 garlic cloves, minced
2 teaspoons minced ginger
2 tablespoons pine nuts
1 cup washed quinoa
2 cups low-sodium chicken or vegetable broth
  Sea salt and freshly ground black pepper
¼ cup chopped fresh parsley

Heat the oil in a large nonstick sauté pan over medium heat.

Add the onion, bell pepper, carrot, garlic, ginger, and pine nuts. Cook until the onions are soft but not brown, about 4 minutes.

Add the quinoa and cook for 1 minute.

Stir in the broth and season to taste with salt and pepper. Bring to a boil over high heat. Reduce the heat to low, cover, and simmer for 20 minutes or until the quinoa is tender and the broth is absorbed.

Add the parsley, and fluff the quinoa with a fork before serving.

ROASTED BALSAMIC RADICCHIO

Serves 4

- 3 tablespoons extra-virgin olive oil
- 2 garlic cloves, minced
- ¼ cup balsamic vinegar
- 1 tablespoon chopped fresh thyme
  Sea salt and freshly ground black pepper
- 2 large heads radicchio, halved through the root
  Grated Parmesan or pecorino Romano cheese, as garnish

To prepare the marinade, combine the oil, garlic, vinegar, and thyme in a large bowl, mixing well. Add salt and pepper to taste.

Add the radicchio, tossing gently to coat well. Marinate for 1 hour at room temperature.

Preheat oven to 450°F.

Place the radicchio wedges in a baking pan and pour the marinade over the wedges.

Roast in the oven until the edges of the radicchio are crisp and just tender when pierced with a knife, about 20 minutes.

Top with cheese and serve at once.

LEMON-MINT COUSCOUS

Serves 4

2 teaspoons olive oil
2 shallots, finely chopped
1 box (10 ounces) whole wheat couscous
2 cups low-sodium chicken or vegetable broth
⅓ cup finely chopped mint
   Zest of 1 lemon, finely chopped
2 tablespoons freshly squeezed lemon juice
   Sea salt and freshly ground black pepper

Heat the oil in a 2- to 3-quart nonstick saucepan over medium heat. Add the shallots and cook, stirring occasionally, until the shallots are translucent but not brown, 3 to 5 minutes.

Add the couscous; stir to coat with oil.

Add the broth, cover, and reduce heat to low. Cook, stirring occasionally, until the couscous is soft and all the liquid has been absorbed, about 15 minutes. Remove the couscous from the heat.

Stir in the mint, lemon zest, and lemon juice. Season to taste with salt and pepper.

MEAT

GINGER-BEEF STIR FRY
WITH BABY BOK CHOY

Serves 4

2   tablespoons dry sherry
2   tablespoons hoisin sauce
2   tablespoons grated ginger
1   tablespoon oyster sauce
2   teaspoons Asian sesame oil
½   teaspoon chili paste
2   garlic cloves, minced
1   pound flank steak
1   tablespoon canola oil
1   pound baby bok choy, cleaned and sliced
¼   cup low-sodium chicken broth
    Hot rice or soba noodles
1   green onion, finely minced, as garnish
    Toasted sesame seeds, as garnish

To prepare the marinade, combine the sherry, hoisin sauce, ginger, oyster sauce, sesame oil, chili paste, and garlic in a small bowl.

Cut the flank steak across the grain into thin slices. (Place meat in the freezer for 30 minutes to make cutting easier.) Toss the meat with the marinade, and marinate for 15 minutes to 1 hour. Drain, reserving the marinade.

Heat the canola oil in a nonstick wok over high heat. Add the beef and stir-fry for 2 minutes. Using a slotted spoon, transfer the beef to a platter.

Reduce heat to medium high and add the bok choy; stir-fry for 2 minutes.

Add the chicken broth and the reserved marinade to the skillet, tossing well. Bring to a boil and stir-fry until the bok choy is tender, 2 minutes.

Add the beef to the skillet and stir-fry until the sauce is reduced a bit, about 2 minutes.

Serve over hot rice or soba noodles; garnish with green onion and sesame seeds.

VARIATION Substitute Chinese broccoli, snow pea pods, broccoli rabe, broccoli, or greens for the bok choy.

RECOMMENDED WINE
Zinfandel Ghirardelli Vineyard 2003
Milliaire Winery • Murphys, California

ALTERNATIVES
Zinfandel or *Syrah*

BEEF FAJITAS

Serves 4

¼ cup fresh lime juice
¼ cup minced cilantro
2 garlic cloves
½ teaspoon ground cumin
½ teaspoon ground coriander
½ jalapeño chili, seeded and chopped
1 pound flank steak or skirt steak
2 teaspoons olive oil
  Salt and pepper
1 large onion, thinly sliced
1 red bell pepper, seeded and thinly sliced
1 green bell pepper, seeded and thinly sliced
4 whole wheat tortillas
1 avocado, sliced
½ cup low-fat sour cream or yogurt
1 cup salsa
1 fresh lime, cut into wedges

In a small bowl, combine the lime juice, cilantro, garlic, cumin, coriander, and jalapeño. Pour the mixture over the steak; allow it to marinate for 30 minutes to 1 hour.

Heat the oil in a nonstick sauté pan over high heat. Add the steak; season with salt and pepper, and cook until it is the desired degree of doneness, 2 to 3 minutes per side. Transfer the steak to a cutting surface and allow it to stand for 5 minutes.

Reduce the heat to medium high. Add a bit more olive oil to the pan if necessary. Add the onions and bell peppers; cook, stirring frequently, until the onions start to get soft, about 5 minutes.

Slice the meat against the grain into thin slices.

Serve the beef with warmed tortillas, the bell pepper mixture, avocado, sour cream, salsa, and lime wedges.

RECOMMENDED WINE
Napa Valley Meritage 2003
Casa Nuestra Winery • St. Helena, California

ALTERNATIVES
Cabernet Sauvignon or *Cabernet Franc*

TUSCAN BEEF STEW

Serves 6

1 tablespoon olive oil
3 pounds boneless beef chuck, trimmed and cut into 2-inch cubes
2 large onions, chopped
4 garlic cloves, minced
2 bay leaves
1 teaspoon salt
½ teaspoon freshly grated black pepper
2 tablespoons tomato paste
1½ cups dry red wine
2 cups tomato sauce
2 tablespoons chopped fresh sage
2 tablespoons chopped fresh oregano
2 tablespoons chopped fresh parsley, as garnish
¼ cup grated Parmesan, as garnish

Preheat oven to 350°F.

Heat the oil over medium-high heat in a deep ovenproof skillet (large enough to hold the meat in one layer). Add the meat and cook, stirring occasionally, until all the juices have evaporated and the meat is browned, 20 to 25 minutes.

Reduce the heat to medium. Stir in the onion, garlic, bay leaves, salt, and pepper. Cook until the onion is soft but not brown, about 3 minutes.

Stir in the tomato paste, cook for 1 additional minute. Add the wine; bring to a boil and cover tightly.

Bake in the oven until the meat is tender and almost all of the wine has evaporated, about 1 hour. Stir in the tomato sauce, sage, and oregano; return the pan to the oven. Continue baking until the meat is soft enough to cut with a spoon, about 1 hour longer.

Serve garnished with parsley and cheese.

NOTES Serve with creamy polenta or whole wheat pasta and sautéed greens. Use leftovers as a pasta sauce.

VARIATION Add assorted seasonal vegetables the last hour of cooking: carrots, potatoes, peppers, etc.

RECOMMENDED WINE
Barolo Sarmassa 1999
Brezza Giacomo e Figli ◆ Barolo, Italy

ALTERNATIVES
Nebbiolo or *Sangiovese*

VEAL OSSO BUCCO

Serves 4

4 organic veal shanks or lamb shanks
  Sea salt and freshly ground pepper
2 tablespoons olive oil
1 cup diced onion (¼-inch pieces)
1 cup diced celery (¼-inch pieces)
1 cup diced carrot (¼-inch pieces)
½ cup whole garlic cloves
1 cup pinot noir or other dry red wine
1 tablespoon soy sauce
1 cup beef or veal stock (homemade is best)
1 teaspoon whole peppercorns
1 bay leaf
1 medium orange, peeled and very thinly sliced
1 tablespoon arrowroot
1 tablespoon water

Preheat oven to 350°F.

Season four veal shanks with salt and pepper.

Heat a dutch oven or other ovenproof pan over medium heat. (The pan should be big enough for the shanks to fit comfortably, not tight but not too much space around them.) Add the olive oil and heat until hot but not smoking. Add the veal shanks and brown well on both sides. Remove from the pan and set aside.

Add the onion, celery, carrot, and garlic to the pan. Sauté over medium heat, stirring frequently, until they begin to brown.

Add the wine and soy sauce, stirring to scrape up the browned bits from the bottom of the pan. Return the veal shanks to the pan, nestling them into the browned vegetables.

Add the stock, peppercorns, and bay leaf. Cover the top with the orange slices. The shanks should be almost covered; if not, add a bit more stock.

Cover tightly with a lid or foil, and bake until tender, 1½ to 2 hours. Let rest for 15 or 20 minutes.

Prepare a slurry by combining the arrowroot and water. Remove the shanks; thicken the sauce over medium heat with the arrowroot slurry. Add a little at a time, stirring constantly, until the sauce coats a spoon. Adjust seasoning, and salt and pepper to taste.

Serve shanks topped with sauce.

Courtesy of Richard Gehrts, Red Hills Provincial Dining, Dundee, Oregon

---

RECOMMENDED WINE
Temperance Hill Vineyard Pinot Noir 2003
Torri Mor Winery ♦ Dundee, Oregon

ALTERNATIVES
Pinot Noir or *Sangiovese*

HARIRA (MOROCCAN LAMB STEW)

Serves 4 to 6

¼ cup olive oil
1 chopped Walla Walla or other sweet onion
5 large garlic cloves, chopped
1 teaspoon ground cinnamon
1 teaspoon turmeric
2 tablespoons top quality curry powder
1 pound lamb shoulder, cubed
1 can (15 ounces) minced tomatoes with juice
2 cups low-sodium beef broth
1 cup cabernet or other dry red wine
1 can (14 ounces) chickpeas, drained and rinsed
2 beaten eggs
    Juice of 2 lemons
    Couscous, prepared
    Chopped parsley, as garnish
    Chopped cilantro, as garnish
    Lemon zest, as garnish

Heat the oil in a large heavy stockpot over medium heat. Add the onion and sauté until it starts to brown, about 5 minutes. Add the garlic and cook for 1 minute; add the cinnamon, turmeric, and curry powder, and cook for 1 additional minute.

Add the lamb, coating it completely with the spice mixture, and cook it for 3 minutes.

Stir in the tomatoes with juice, beef broth, and wine, and bring to a boil. Reduce heat to a simmer and cook for 30 minutes.

In a small bowl, mash half of the chickpeas. Add the mashed and whole chickpeas to the stew and continue to cook, stirring occasionally, 1 hour. At the end of 1 hour, swirl in the beaten eggs to form long strands. Stir in the lemon juice.

Serve over couscous; garnish with parsley, cilantro, and lemon zest.

Courtesy of Dr. & Mrs. Joe Gunselman, Spokane, Washington

RECOMMENDED WINE
Columbia Valley Claret 2003
Robert Karl Cellars • Spokane, Washington

ALTERNATIVES
Syrah or *Petit Sirah*

GREEK LAMB SHANKS
WITH ORZO AND FETA
Serves 4

1 tablespoon extra-virgin olive oil
4 lamb shanks
   Sea salt and freshly ground pepper
2 large onions, sliced
4 large garlic cloves, minced
2 cups low-sodium chicken stock
1 cup dry white wine
1 tablespoon chopped fresh rosemary
1 tablespoon chopped fresh thyme
1 tablespoon chopped fresh oregano
1 cup orzo
1 cup crumbled feta cheese
2 tablespoons chopped parsley

In a large dutch oven, heat the oil over medium-high heat. Add the shanks and brown well on all sides, sprinkling with salt and pepper. Remove to a warm plate.

Reduce heat to medium, add the onions to the pan, and cook until soft, about 5 minutes.

Stir in the garlic, stock, wine, rosemary, thyme, and oregano.

Put the shanks back into the pan and bring to boil. Reduce heat, cover, and simmer until meat is very tender, about 3 hours.

Raise heat to medium. Add orzo and cook, uncovered, until the orzo is done, about 15 minutes.

Sprinkle with feta cheese and parsley before serving.

Adapted from a recipe from the New Zealand Lamb Cooperative

RECOMMENDED WINE
Ehlers Estate Cabernet Franc 2003
Ehlers Estate ◆ St. Helena, California

ALTERNATIVES
Cabernet Franc or *Syrah*

ASIAN-MARINATED RACK OF LAMB
Serves 2

Marinade
⅓ cup hoisin sauce
¼ cup toasted sesame seeds
2 tablespoons soy sauce
3 tablespoons sweet chili sauce
2 tablespoons minced garlic
1 tablespoon Asian sesame oil
1 tablespoon minced ginger
1 tablespoon grated orange zest
1 tablespoon fermented black beans, rinsed and drained
2 teaspoons good quality curry powder

Lamb
1 rack (2 pounds) of lamb
   Chopped fresh cilantro, as garnish

To prepare the marinade: Combine all of the ingredients, mixing well.

To prepare the lamb: Place the rack of lamb in a stainless steel or glass bowl and pour the marinade over it; coat evenly. Marinate for at least 2 hours. Bring to room temperature prior to cooking.

Prepare a barbecue or indoor grill. Grill the rack of lamb, turning it occasionally and brushing on more sauce until the meat is medium rare in the center. (Alternatively, roast in a 400°F oven until the meat registers 145°F.) Slice the rack into chops; divide between two plates. Serve at once, topped with chopped cilantro.

RECOMMENDED WINE
Bergström Vineyard Pinot Noir 2004
Bergström Winery • Newberg, Oregon

ALTERNATIVES
Pinot Noir or *Syrah*

LAMB CHOPS WITH YOGURT-MINT SAUCE

Serves 4

¾ cup plain yogurt
¼ cup finely chopped mint leaves
1 garlic clove, minced
  Dash of cayenne
4 rib lamb chops, 1 inch thick
  Herbes de Provence
  Sea salt and freshly ground black pepper
1 tablespoon extra-virgin olive oil

Stir together the yogurt, mint, garlic, and cayenne to taste. Set aside.

Pat the lamb chops dry. Season with herbes de Provence; salt and pepper to taste.

Heat the oil in a 12-inch skillet (preferably cast iron) over medium-high heat until hot but not smoking. Add the chops and sauté 3 minutes per side for medium rare.

Serve topped with the yogurt sauce.

RECOMMENDED WINE
Napa Valley Petite Sirah,
Pickett Road Vineyards 2003
Rosenblum Cellars • Alameda, California

ALTERNATIVES
Petit Sirah or *Syrah*

VENISON WITH CHERRY-GINGER SAUCE

Serves 6 to 8

 2 tablespoons finely chopped fresh rosemary
 1 tablespoon coriander seeds, toasted
 4 garlic cloves, minced
 2 venison tenderloins, 1 pound each
 2 tablespoons olive oil
   Kosher salt and freshly ground black pepper
 2 teaspoons cornstarch
 2 cups low-sodium beef or chicken broth
 1 cup dry red wine
1½ cups dried tart cherries
 1 tablespoon grated ginger
 1 tablespoon grated orange zest
 1 tablespoon honey

Using a spice grinder, combine the rosemary, coriander, and garlic to make a paste.

Rub each tenderloin with 1 tablespoon of the olive oil, then rub each tenderloin with the paste. Cover and refrigerate for 30 minutes.

Preheat oven to 450°F.

Heat the remaining 1 tablespoon of olive oil in an ovenproof nonstick sauté pan over high heat. Add the tenderloin and cook until browned, turning once, about 5 minutes. Season with salt and pepper.

Place in the oven; roast until a meat thermometer registers 125°F, 8 to 10 minutes.

Transfer the meat to plate and cover with foil.

Stir the cornstarch into a bit of the broth until smooth. Add the cornstarch mixture, wine, cherries, ginger, orange zest, and remaining broth to the sauté pan over medium-high heat, stirring with a wooden spoon to loosen any browned bits on the bottom of the pan. Simmer until thickened, about 5 minutes. Whisk in the honey, and season to taste with salt and pepper.

Slice the venison on the diagonal, and serve with the sauce.

RECOMMENDED WINE
Napa Valley Argos Meritage 2002
Dutch Henry Winery ◆ Calistoga, California

ALTERNATIVES
Merlot or *Cabernet Sauvignon*

PORK LOIN STUFFED
WITH SAGE AND ROSEMARY

Serves 4

Filling

2	tablespoons chopped parsley
1½	tablespoons chopped fresh sage
1	tablespoon chopped fresh rosemary
3	garlic cloves, minced
2	tablespoons extra-virgin olive oil
2	teaspoons Dijon mustard
¼	teaspoon salt
¼	teaspoon freshly ground black pepper

Pork Loin

2	pounds boneless center loin pork roast
¾	teaspoon salt
1	teaspoon freshly ground black pepper
1	tablespoon extra-virgin olive oil
	Fresh sage leaves, as garnish
	Fresh rosemary, as garnish

Preheat oven to 350°F.

To prepare the filling: Combine all the filling ingredients in a small bowl and set aside.

To prepare the pork loin: Butterfly the pork loin, cutting the roast horizontally to within ¼ inch of the other side. Sprinkle the top portion with half of the salt and pepper. Spread the filling evenly across the loin, leaving a ½-inch border.

Beginning at the opposite edge, roll the loin to wrap the filling. Using kitchen twine, tie the loin every 1½ inches to hold the shape.

Rub the loin with oil, and sprinkle it with the remaining salt and pepper. Place the loin in a small roasting pan and position it on the center rack of the oven.

Roast for 1 hour or until a thermometer registers 155°F. Let stand 10 minutes before carving.

Serve with fresh sage leaves and rosemary as garnish.

Courtesy of Dr. & Mrs. Joe Gunselman, Spokane, Washington

RECOMMENDED WINE
Barolo Cannubi 2000
Fratelli Serio e Battista Borgogno • Barolo, Italy

ALTERNATIVES
Cabernet Sauvignon or *Merlot*

SPICE-RUBBED PORK CHOPS

Serves 4

1 tablespoon ground cumin
1 tablespoon ground coriander
1 tablespoon sweet paprika
1 teaspoon curry powder
4 boneless pork loin chops, ¾-inch thick
1 teaspoon salt
½ teaspoon freshly ground black pepper
1 tablespoon extra-virgin olive oil
3 garlic cloves, minced
  Juice and finely grated zest of 1 lime
¼ cup chopped cilantro

Preheat oven to 400°F.

In a small bowl, combine the cumin, coriander, paprika, and curry powder.

Pat the pork chops dry, and season with salt and pepper. Rub the cumin mixture into both sides of the chops.

Heat the olive oil in a large ovenproof skillet over high heat. Brown the chops, about 1 minute on each side.

Stir in the garlic, lime juice and zest, and cilantro, and roast the chops in the oven until just cooked through, about 10 to 15 minutes.

RECOMMENDED WINE
Napa Zinfandel 2003
T-Vine Cellars • Calistoga, California

ALTERNATIVES
Zinfandel or *Syrah*

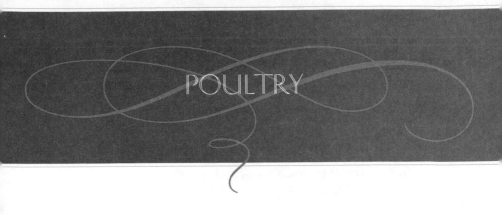

FOURTEEN

POULTRY

PARMESAN-CRUSTED CHICKEN
WITH WILD GREENS SALAD

Serves 4

Chicken

2 tablespoons Dijon mustard
1 tablespoon olive oil
1 tablespoon chopped fresh basil
1 tablespoon chopped fresh oregano
4 boneless chicken breast halves, 6 ounces each, skinless
   Salt and freshly ground black pepper
¾ cup grated Parmesan cheese

Salad

6 cups mixed wild greens
1 cup cherry tomatoes, halved
   Balsamic vinegar
   Extra-virgin olive oil
   Salt and pepper

Preheat oven to 450°F.

To prepare the chicken: Combine the Dijon mustard, olive oil, basil, and oregano. Season the chicken with salt and pepper, then rub the mustard mixture over both sides of the chicken. Put the Parmesan cheese on a plate and roll each chicken breast in the cheese, pressing lightly. Transfer the chicken to a baking dish.

Bake the chicken until just cooked through and browned, about 15 minutes.

To prepare the salad: In a large bowl, combine the greens and tomatoes; drizzle with balsamic vinegar and olive oil to taste, and season with salt and pepper.

Divide the salad mixture among four plates, top with the chicken, and serve.

RECOMMENDED WINE
Io 2002
Byron Vineyard and Winery
Santa Maria, California

ALTERNATIVES
Grenache or *Malbec*

ASIAN CHICKEN LETTUCE WRAPS

Serves 4

2 pounds boneless chicken breast, skinless
  Salt and freshly ground black pepper
1 tablespoon canola oil
2 tablespoons minced ginger root
4 garlic cloves, minced
1 large red bell pepper, seeded and thinly sliced
1 cup packaged shredded cabbage and carrot mix
2 scallions, sliced
¼ cup sweet chili sauce
¼ cup hoisin sauce
1 cup basil leaves
1 tablespoon fish sauce
½ head leaf lettuce (4 leaves)
¼ cup chopped fresh mint
1 cup bean sprouts
2 tablespoons chopped peanuts

Slice the chicken into thin strips and season to taste with salt and pepper.

Heat the oil in a large nonstick skillet over high heat until almost smoking. Add the chicken and cook for 2 minutes, stirring constantly.

Add the ginger, garlic, bell pepper, cabbage and carrot mix, and scallions, and stir-fry for another 2 minutes.

Add the chili sauce and hoisin sauce to glaze the mixture; toss for 1 minute. Add the basil and cook until the leaves are just wilted. Add the fish sauce, turning to coat. Transfer the cooked chicken and vegetables to a bowl.

To serve, place a quarter of the chicken mixture on each lettuce leaf; top each with a quarter of the mint, bean sprouts, and peanuts. Fold the lettuce over to eat (like a small taco).

RECOMMENDED WINE
Edizione Pennino Zinfandel 2003
Rubicon Estate • Rutherford, California

ALTERNATIVES
Zinfandel or *Syrah*

CHICKEN BREASTS STUFFED WITH ARTICHOKES AND GOAT CHEESE

Serves 4

Stuffing

- 2 teaspoons extra-virgin olive oil
- 1 tablespoon chopped fresh thyme, or 1 teaspoon dried
- ¼ teaspoon crushed red pepper flakes
- ¾ cup artichoke hearts, drained and coarsely chopped
- 2 garlic cloves, minced
- 4 ounces crumbled goat cheese or feta cheese
- 2 tablespoons chopped and pitted black Greek olives
- 2 tablespoons chopped oil-packed sun-dried tomatoes
- 2 tablespoons chopped fresh basil
  Salt and freshly ground black pepper

Chicken

- 4 boneless chicken breasts, 6- to 8-ounces each, skinless
- 2 teaspoons extra-virgin olive oil
  Salt and freshly ground black pepper
- 1 tablespoon chopped fresh thyme, or 1 teaspoon dried
- 2 cups low-sodium chicken broth
  Juice and finely minced zest of 1 lemon
- 2 teaspoons cornstarch
  Chopped fresh parsley, as garnish

To prepare the stuffing: Heat the olive oil in a nonstick sauté pan over medium heat. Add the thyme and red pepper flakes, and cook for 1 minute. Add the artichoke hearts and garlic, and cook for 2 to 3 minutes, stirring occasionally. Remove from heat and stir in the goat cheese, olives, sun-dried tomatoes, and basil. Season to taste with salt and pepper, and allow to cool.

To prepare the chicken: Rinse the chicken breasts and pat them dry with paper towels. Place each breast between two sheets of plastic wrap and pound to flatten evenly to ¼-inch thickness.

Spread each breast with a quarter of the stuffing. Fold the breasts in half over the stuffing and use toothpicks to securely close the sides.

Heat the olive oil in a large nonstick skillet over medium heat. Add the chicken, season to taste with salt and pepper, and sauté for 6 minutes on each side or until done. Remove from pan and cover to keep warm.

Add the thyme, broth, and lemon zest to the pan; bring to a boil. Combine the lemon juice and cornstarch; add it to the broth mixture, stirring with a whisk. Cook until thick, about 1 minute.

Return the chicken to the pan; cover and cook for 2 minutes or until thoroughly heated.

Serve garnished with fresh parsley, if desired.

RECOMMENDED WINE
Fume Blanc Napa Valley 2005
Robert Mondavi Winery • Oakville, California

ALTERNATIVES
Sauvignon Blanc or *Chardonnay*

MOROCCAN GRILLED CHICKEN
WITH MINT SAUCE

Serves 4

4 6-ounce boneless chicken breasts, skinless

Marinade

1 cup plain whole milk yogurt
   Juice and zest of 1 lemon
2 garlic cloves, minced
1 small onion, minced
1 teaspoon ground cumin
1 teaspoon ground coriander
1 teaspoon chili powder
1 teaspoon salt
½ teaspoon black pepper
¼ teaspoon cinnamon

Sauce

1 cup plain whole-milk yogurt
½ cup chopped fresh mint leaves

Rinse the chicken and pat it dry.

To prepare the marinade: Whisk together all the marinade ingredients.

In a large bowl, pour the marinade over the chicken; marinate at room temperature for 30 minutes.

While the chicken is marinating, prepare the grill for cooking.

Grill the chicken, turning occasionally, until just cooked through, about 5 to 6 minutes per side. Remove to a platter and let rest for 10 minutes. Discard the marinade.

To prepare the sauce: Combine the yogurt and mint in a small bowl.

Slice the chicken on the diagonal and drizzle the chicken with yogurt sauce.

RECOMMENDED WINE
The Holy Trinity 2001
Grant Burge Wines, Ltd
Jacobs Creek, Barossa Valley, South Australia

ALTERNATIVES
Grenache or *Syrah*

CHICKEN BREASTS
WITH FRESH MOZZARELLA

Serves 4

4 boneless chicken breasts, 6 ounces each, skinless
  Salt and freshly ground black pepper
2 tablespoons olive oil
3 garlic cloves, minced
1 cup dry white wine
12 fresh basil leaves
8 ounces fresh mozzarella, cut into 8 slices

Rinse the chicken and pat it dry. Season to taste with salt and pepper.

Heat the olive oil in a large skillet over medium heat; add the garlic. Add the chicken breasts and cook until golden brown on both sides and almost cooked through, turning as necessary, about 6 to 10 minutes. Transfer to a plate and keep warm.

Add the wine to the pan, scraping to release any browned bits on the bottom of the pan, and simmer briefly to reduce the sauce by half. Return the chicken to the pan and cook for 1 minute.

Top each chicken breast with 3 basil leaves and 2 slices of mozzarella. Cover the pan and remove it from the heat. Set it aside for a few minutes until the mozzarella softens and begins to melt. Sprinkle the chicken with additional salt and pepper to taste.

Serve the chicken on heated plates, topped with the sauce.

RECOMMENDED WINE
Viongier/Roussanne 2004
Kinkead Ridge Vineyard and Estate Winery
Ripley, Ohio

ALTERNATIVES
Viognier or *Roussanne*

CHICKEN POACHED IN ORANGE JUICE AND FRESH ROSEMARY

Serves 4

4 boneless chicken breasts, 6 ounces each, skinless
  Salt and freshly ground black pepper
4 large sprigs fresh rosemary
2 cups freshly squeezed orange juice
⅓ cup balsamic vinegar
2 tablespoons finely minced orange zest
½ cup currants, rinsed and well drained, as garnish
1 cup coarsely chopped walnuts, toasted, as garnish

Preheat oven to 375°F.

Rinse the chicken and pat it dry with paper towels. Season to taste with salt and pepper.

Place the chicken breasts in a single layer in a glass baking dish. Place a rosemary sprig under each breast. Pour orange juice over the chicken. Cover and cook for about 12 minutes, or until an instant-read thermometer registers 165°F. Be careful not to overcook. When the chicken is done, arrange it on a serving platter, discarding the rosemary.

Whisk the balsamic vinegar and orange zest into the cooking juices and adjust seasoning. Pour the sauce over the chicken. Garnish with currants and walnuts.

VARIATIONS Substitute raisins for currants, or hazelnuts for walnuts.

RECOMMENDED WINE
Pinot Noir 2002
Arger-Martucci Vineyards
St. Helena, California

ALTERNATIVES
Pinot Noir or *Sauvignon Blanc*

MOROCCAN GAME HENS

Serves 4

NOTE The hens should marinate for at least 12 hours, so begin preparation a day before serving.

 1 large orange (unpeeled), thinly sliced
 2 Cornish game hens, cut in half lengthwise
 ¼ cup chopped fresh cilantro, plus 2 tablespoons for garnish
 8 garlic cloves, finely chopped
 1 teaspoon ground cumin
 1 teaspoon ground coriander
 1 teaspoon curry powder
 ¼ cup low-sodium chicken stock
 ¼ cup orange juice
 2 tablespoons olive oil
 3 tablespoons balsamic vinegar
 1 tablespoon wildflower honey
10 whole pitted dates
10 large pitted green olives
    Sea salt and freshly ground black pepper

Sauce
 1 teaspoon ground cumin
 1 teaspoon ground coriander
    Sea salt and freshly ground black pepper

To prepare the hens for marinating, one day before serving: Arrange the orange slices in the bottom of a 9″ × 13″ glass baking dish. Top the orange slices with the game hens. Mix ¼ cup of the fresh cilantro, the garlic, cumin, coriander, and curry powder in a bowl. Rub the mixture all over the hens.

In a small bowl, whisk together the chicken stock, orange juice, oil, vinegar, and honey. Pour the mixture over the hens. Tuck the dates and olives between the hens. Season to taste with salt and pepper. Cover and refrigerate at least 12 hours or overnight, turning the hens once.

To cook the hens: Preheat oven to 375°F.

Arrange the hens skin side up. Bake the hens with the marinade, dates, and olives until the hens are cooked through, basting occasionally, about 50 minutes. Transfer the hens, dates, and olives to a platter; discard the orange slices.

To prepare the sauce: Pour the pan juices into a small heavy saucepan. Add the cumin and coriander. Boil until reduced to ½ cup, whisking frequently, about 5 minutes. Season with salt and pepper.

Spoon some sauce over the hens. Garnish with the remaining 2 tablespoons of chopped cilantro. Serve, passing the remaining sauce separately.

RECOMMENDED WINE
Cabernet Franc 2003
Kenefick Ranch • Calistoga, California

ALTERNATIVES
Cabernet Franc or *Syrah*

HERB-ROASTED PHEASANT BREASTS

Serves 4

4 pheasant breasts, including skin and bone

Stuffing

4 ounces pepper Boursin cheese

½ cup smoky bacon or pancetta, sliced (optional)

4 garlic cloves, minced

¼ cup chopped fresh rosemary

¼ cup chopped fresh oregano

¼ cup chopped fresh thyme

¼ cup chopped fresh sage

1 whole lemon (including rind), finely diced

1 teaspoon salt

¼ teaspoon pepper

Preheat oven to 400°F.

Loosen the skin from the pheasant breasts.

To prepare the stuffing: Combine all of the ingredients for the stuffing, mixing well.

To prepare the pheasant: Spread a thin layer of the stuffing (about one third of the mixture) between the skin and the meat of each piece.

Place the pheasant breasts in a nonstick baking dish sprayed with oil. Place the remaining stuffing on top of the pheasant. (If the pheasant is skinless, all of the stuffing can be placed directly on top of the meat.)

Bake until the meat is just cooked through, about 15 to 18 minutes. Time will vary according to the size of the pheasants. Do not overcook.

VARIATION   Substitute crumbled feta or goat cheese for the pepper Boursin cheese.

RECOMMENDED WINE

Napa Valley Merlot 2003

Duckhorn Vineyards ◆ St. Helena, California

ALTERNATIVES

Merlot or *Syrah*

SAUTÉED DUCK BREAST WITH MUSHROOM SAUCE

Serves 4

- 4 boneless duck breast halves, 6 ounces each, with skin
  Sea salt and freshly ground black pepper
- 1 tablespoon olive oil
- 1½ pounds assorted wild mushrooms (oyster, Portobello, shiitake, porcini), cleaned and thickly sliced
- ¼ cup shallots, thinly sliced
- ½ cup dry red wine
- 2 tablespoons chopped fresh parsley

Preheat oven to 300°F.

Using a sharp knife, score the skin of the duck breasts, pat them dry, and season the duck with salt and pepper.

Heat a large heavy nonstick skillet over high heat, add the duck breasts, skin side down, and cook until the skin is a deep golden brown, about 8 minutes. Turn the duck over, and cook about 3 minutes for medium rare.

Transfer the duck to a baking sheet and keep it warm in the oven.

Pour all fat from the skillet. Add the olive oil, scraping up the pan drippings, and reduce heat to medium high.

Add the mushrooms and shallots, and sauté until the mushrooms are tender, about 8 minutes. Season with salt and pepper. Add the wine; stir until the juices thicken, scraping up the browned bits, about 3 minutes.

Place one duck breast on each of four plates. Pour the mushroom sauce over each, sprinkle with parsley, and serve.

RECOMMENDED WINE
Cabernet Sauvignon 2001
Napa Wine Company ◆ Oakville, California

ALTERNATIVES
Cabernet Sauvignon or *Merlot*

FIFTEEN

FISH AND SHELLFISH

FILLET OF SOLE
WITH PORTOBELLO MUSHROOMS

Serves 4

1 tablespoon canola oil
½ medium onion, coarsely chopped
2 teaspoons freshly squeezed lemon or lime juice
1 tablespoon soy sauce
6 ounces portobello caps, sliced
   Sea salt
1 tablespoon chopped fresh dill or other herbs, or 1 teaspoon dried
4 sole fillets, 6 ounces each

Heat the oil in a large nonstick skillet over medium heat. Add the onion and sauté for about 30 seconds. Add the lemon juice and soy sauce; add the mushrooms, seasoning them lightly with salt. Continue to sauté the mixture, stirring gently the entire time, until the mushrooms become limp and lose their chalk-white appearance. When the mushrooms are very soft, in 10 to 12 minutes, add the fresh dill. Stir for another minute or so.

Season the fillets with salt and place them over the mushroom mixture in the skillet. Cover; cook over medium heat until the fillets are just cooked, 5 to 7 minutes. Serve the fillets topped with portobello mushrooms.

VARIATION Substitute virtually any kind of fish, including oily fish like bluefish or salmon, for use with this portobello topping.

Courtesy of Jack Czarnecki, Joel Palmer House, Dayton, Oregon

RECOMMENDED WINE
Oregon Pinot Gris 2004
Torri Mor Winery • Dundee, Oregon

ALTERNATIVES
Pinot Gris or *Sauvignon Blanc*

ORANGE-CHIPOTLE SCALLOPS

Serves 4

1   tablespoon extra-virgin olive oil
1½ pounds large sea scallops
    Sea salt
1   teaspoon ground cumin
½   cup freshly squeezed orange juice
    Finely minced zest of 1 orange
    Juice and finely minced zest of 1 lime
1   tablespoon minced chipotle in adobo sauce
1   teaspoon honey
1   tablespoon butter
½   cup chopped cilantro

Heat a large nonstick skillet over medium-high heat. Add the olive oil.

Sprinkle the scallops with salt and cumin. Add the scallops to the pan and cook until just browned, about 2 to 3 minutes per side. Remove from the pan and cover to keep warm.

Add the orange juice and zest, lime juice and zest, chipotle, and honey to the pan. Bring to a boil and cook until reduced to ¼ cup. Stir in the butter and cilantro.

Serve the scallops topped with sauce.

RECOMMENDED WINE
Pinot Noir Russian River Valley 2003
Merry Edwards Wines ♦ Windsor, California

ALTERNATIVES
Pinot Noir or *Grenache*

BAKED HALIBUT PROVENÇALE

Serves 4

1 tablespoon olive oil
2 cups chopped white onion
1 cup chopped fennel
2 tablespoons chopped garlic
2 pounds plum tomatoes, peeled, seeded and diced, or 2 cups diced
  and drained canned plum tomatoes
2 tablespoons capers, chopped, rinsed, and drained
1 tablespoon chopped kalamata olives
¼ cup chopped fresh basil
2 tablespoons chopped fresh parsley
1 tablespoon chopped fresh thyme
2 teaspoons anchovy paste
½ teaspoon sea salt
¼ teaspoon freshly ground black pepper
¼ cup dry whole wheat breadcrumbs
3 tablespoons Parmesan cheese
2 tablespoons chopped pine nuts
4 halibut steaks (or other firm-fleshed white fish), 6 ounces each
¼ cup dry red wine

Preheat oven to 350°F.

Heat the olive oil in a large nonstick sauté pan over medium heat. Sauté the onion, fennel, and garlic until soft. Stir in the tomatoes, capers, olives, basil, parsley, thyme, and anchovy paste. Season with salt and pepper.

In a small bowl, combine the breadcrumbs with the Parmesan and pine nuts.

Spray a 9″ × 13″ baking dish with cooking spray. Spread one half of the onion mixture on the bottom of the pan; top evenly with the halibut fillets. Spread the remaining onion mixture over the top of the fish.

Drizzle the wine over the fillets; sprinkle the breadcrumb mixture over the top.

Bake until the fish flakes easily and the topping is brown, 30 to 35 minutes.

RECOMMENDED WINE
Minervois 2002
Château St. Jacques d'Albas ♦ Laure-Minervois, France

ALTERNATIVES
Grenache or *Carignane*

SEA BASS WITH CHILI AND TOMATO

Serves 4

- 1 tablespoon olive oil
- 1 white onion, thinly sliced
- ½ teaspoon red chili flakes
- 4 sea bass fillets (or other white fish), 6 ounces each
  Sea salt and freshly ground black pepper
- 4 ripe tomatoes, peeled, seeded, and diced
- 2 teaspoons grated lemon zest
- 2 cups cooked brown rice
- 16 ounces sautéed spinach
- 2 tablespoons chopped parsley, as garnish

Heat the oil in a large nonstick sauté pan over medium-high heat. Add the onion and chili flakes; cook for 3 minutes.

Sprinkle the fish with salt and pepper; add the fish to the sauté pan. Cook for 4 to 5 minutes on each side until just cooked through. Set aside and keep warm.

Increase heat to high; add the tomatoes and lemon zest to the pan and cook for 3 minutes.

To serve, mix the brown rice and spinach; divide it among four plates. Place the sea bass on top of the rice mixture, drizzle it with the tomato mixture, and garnish with parsley.

RECOMMENDED WINE
Watervale Riesling 2004
Reilly's Wines ♦ Mintaro, South Australia

ALTERNATIVES
Riesling or *Gewürztraminer*

GREEK SHRIMP

Serves 4

- 1 tablespoon olive oil
- 4 large green onions, chopped
- 2 garlic cloves, chopped
- 1 tablespoon chopped fresh oregano, or 1 teaspoon dried
- ½ to 1 teaspoon red pepper flakes
- 1 teaspoon dry mustard
- ½ cup clam juice
- 1 cup white wine
- 2 tablespoons freshly squeezed lemon juice
- 1½ pounds shrimp, peeled and deveined
- ⅔ cup crumbled feta cheese
- ¼ cup chopped parsley

Heat the oil in a large nonstick skillet over medium-high heat. Add the green onions and garlic; sauté for 2 minutes.

Add the oregano, red pepper flakes, dry mustard, clam juice, wine, lemon juice, and shrimp. Cook until the shrimp turns pink.

Remove from heat, and stir in the feta and parsley.

NOTE Serve on a bed of baby spinach or on whole wheat pasta.

RECOMMENDED WINE
Arrowood Viognier, Saralee's Vineyard 2004
Arrowood Vineyards and Winery
Glen Ellen, California

ALTERNATIVES
Viognier or *Riesling*

MEDITERRANEAN FISH STEW

Serves 6

 1   tablespoon olive oil
 1   large onion, chopped
 1   large celery rib, chopped
 1   large carrot, chopped
 4   large garlic cloves, chopped
 ¼   cup chopped parsley
 ¼   cup chopped basil
 1   can (28 ounces) chopped Italian tomatoes with juice
 2   pounds firm white-fleshed fish (halibut, cod, shark, monkfish),
       cut in 2-inch pieces
 1   cup fish stock or clam juice
 1½ cups dry white wine
 1   teaspoon salt
 ½   teaspoon freshly ground black pepper
 ½   teaspoon red chili flakes
 ¼   cup chopped fresh basil, as garnish

Heat the olive oil in large heavy nonstick soup pot over medium-high heat. Add the onion, celery, and carrot; sauté until soft, about 5 minutes.

Add the garlic, parsley, and basil; stir for 1 minute. Add the tomatoes with juice and cook a few minutes longer. Add the fish, fish stock, white wine, salt, pepper, and red chili flakes; simmer until the fish is cooked through, about 10 minutes. Taste and adjust seasonings.

Ladle into bowls and serve; garnish with fresh basil.

RECOMMENDED WINE
Le Mistral 2003
Joseph Phelps Vineyards • St. Helena, California

ALTERNATIVES
Syrah or *Grenache*

SOY-GLAZED SALMON

Serves 4

1 cup reduced-sodium soy sauce
¼ cup honey
½ teaspoon finely minced garlic
4 salmon fillets, 6 ounces each
2 tablespoons sesame seeds

To prepare the glaze, mix the soy sauce, honey, and garlic in a small saucepan, then heat to a simmer over medium-high heat. Cook, stirring occasionally, until the glaze is reduced by about one third, about 7 to 10 minutes.

Pour the glaze into a 9" × 13" baking dish. When the glaze is cool, put the salmon in the dish, skin side up. Marinate for 15 minutes. Turn it over and marinate for another 15 minutes.

Preheat oven to 450°F.

Drain the glaze from the dish and reserve it. Bake the salmon until it is opaque, about 10 minutes.

Brush the salmon with half of the remaining glaze, sprinkle it with sesame seeds, and broil it for 1 to 2 minutes. Drizzle the salmon with the remaining glaze.

NOTE Serve with chopped fresh cabbage and jasmine rice.

RECOMMENDED WINE
Syrah Mount Veeder 2003
Lagier-Meredith Winery • Napa, California

ALTERNATIVES
Syrah or *Merlot*

GARLIC CALAMARI

Serves 6

¼ cup extra-virgin olive oil
1 large yellow onion, julienned
¼ cup chopped garlic
⅓ cup dry white wine
¼ teaspoon salt
¼ teaspoon freshly ground black pepper
   Dash of cayenne
24 ounces cleaned and sliced calamari, with tentacles

Heat the oil in a large sauté pan over medium heat. Sauté the onions until soft; add the garlic and cook for 2 minutes. Add the white wine and cook until the liquid is reduced by one half.

Add the salt, pepper, and cayenne; stir. Add the calamari and toss to coat with the onion mixture. Cover the pan and cook for 2 minutes or until the calamari is opaque.

NOTE Serve with baby mixed greens.

Courtesy of Ghini's French Caffe, Tucson, Arizona

RECOMMENDED WINE
Merlot Napa Valley 2003
Shafer Vineyards • Napa, California

ALTERNATIVES
Merlot or *Chardonnay*

TUNA–BLACK BEAN TOSTADA WITH WATERMELON SLAW AND TOMATILLO SALSA

Serves 6

Tostadas

6   corn tortillas, 4 inches in diameter
3   cups canned black beans, drained and rinsed
2   teaspoons cumin
6   pieces of ahi tuna, 4 ounces each
3   tablespoons extra-virgin olive oil
    Sea salt
    Freshly ground black pepper
    Watermelon Slaw (see recipe on the following page)
    Tomatillo Salsa (see recipe on the following page)
6   ounces crumbled feta cheese
3   tablespoons pumpkin seeds, toasted

Preheat oven to 350°F.

Place the tortillas in single layer on a cookie sheet and bake for 15 minutes until crisp and firm. Set aside.

In a small bowl, combine the black beans with cumin, mashing the beans to achieve a coarse texture. Heat the bean mixture in a small saucepan, then set aside and cover to keep warm.

Brush the tuna with olive oil, and season to taste with salt and pepper. Sear the fish in a hot pan or grill over a hot fire until medium rare, 2 to 4 minutes, depending on the thickness of the fish.

To serve, spread the tortillas with the black beans; top with a portion of fish and some of the Watermelon Slaw. Drizzle Tomatillo Salsa over the top, and sprinkle with feta cheese and pumpkin seeds. Serve additional salsa on the side.

VARIATION   Cumin-Scented Black Beans (see recipe on page 257) can be used instead of the canned black beans and cumin.

(continued)

Watermelon Slaw

    Juice of 1 lime
- ½ teaspoon salt
- ¼ teaspoon freshly ground black pepper
- 2 tablespoons extra-virgin olive oil
- 2 cups watermelon pieces, cut from rind and diced
- 2 cups stemmed watercress
- 1 to 2 jalapeño, Fresno, or serrano chilies, stemmed
- 3 green onions, minced (white and tender green parts only)

To prepare a lime vinaigrette, combine the lime juice, salt, and pepper in a small bowl. Whisk in the oil.

In a separate bowl, combine the watermelon, watercress, chilies, and green onions. Reserve until ready to use. Just before serving, dress with the lime vinaigrette.

NOTES Slice jalapeños at an angle. If you prefer a milder slaw, seed the jalapeños.

Tomatillo Salsa

- 3 serrano chilies, stemmed and seeded
- 1¼ pounds tomatillos, husked
- 2 tablespoons extra-virgin olive oil
- ¼ cup chopped onion
- 1½ teaspoons minced garlic
- ½ teaspoon salt
- ¼ teaspoon freshly ground black pepper
- ¼ cup minced cilantro

Place the chilies and tomatillos in a pot with just enough water to cover. Bring to a boil over high heat, then reduce to a simmer. Cook until just tender, 3 to 5 minutes, depending on how ripe your tomatillos are.

In the meantime, heat the olive oil in a sauté pan over medium heat, add the onion and garlic, and sauté until translucent.

Once the tomatillos and chilies have softened, combine them with the onion mixture, salt, and pepper. Process in a food processor until smooth; strain if desired. Set aside until needed.

Just before serving, mince the cilantro and stir it into the salsa.

Cumin-Scented Black Beans

3 cups dried black beans
2 onions, diced
4 bay leaves
1 guajillo chili
1 árbol chili
3 tablespoons extra-virgin olive oil
3 garlic cloves, chopped
2 tablespoons cumin seeds, toasted

Soak the dried beans in water and cover for 12 hours or overnight.

Drain the beans, rinse, and cover with water. Add half of the diced onion along with the bay leaves and chilies. Bring to a boil, then simmer until tender. Strain and reserve the liquid.

While the beans are cooking, heat the olive oil in a sauté pan over medium heat; add the remainder of the onion, the garlic, and the cumin seeds, and sauté until the onions are softened. Add 2 cups of the cooked beans and some of the reserved liquid; sauté until the liquid is reduced by one half.

Put the mixture into a food processor and pulse two or three times; keep a coarse texture. (Alternatively, mash the bean mixture in a bowl.)

RECOMMENDED WINE
Sauvignon Blanc Napa Valley 2003
Duckhorn Vineyards ◆ St. Helena, California

ALTERNATIVES
Sauvignon Blanc or *Riesling*

ASIAN FISH EN PAPILLOTE

Serves 2

Topping mixture

½ cup sake
¼ cup finely chopped cilantro
2 whole green onions, chopped
2 garlic cloves, minced
1 tablespoon grated ginger
1 tablespoon canola oil
2 teaspoons soy sauce
1 teaspoon fish sauce
1 teaspoon dark sesame oil
½ teaspoon chili garlic sauce

Vegetables and fish

1 cup sliced shiitake mushrooms
2 pieces baby bok choy
½ cup julienned celery
½ cup julienned peeled carrot
½ cup julienned red bell pepper
   Sea salt and freshly ground black pepper
2 fillets of mahi mahi or other white fish, 6 ounces each

Preheat oven to 400°F.

Cut two 12-inch squares of parchment or foil for use in wrapping the rafts of vegetables.

To prepare the topping mixture: In a small bowl, combine the sake, cilantro, green onions, garlic, ginger, oil, soy sauce, fish sauce, sesame oil, and chili garlic sauce. Whisk to combine.

To prepare the vegetables and fish: In a separate bowl, combine the mushrooms, baby bok choy, celery, carrot, and bell pepper.

Make a raft of the combined vegetables in the middle of each of the prepared squares. Season all layers with salt and pepper. Place 1 fillet on top of each raft. Pour the topping mixture over each fillet, dividing it evenly. Form a sealed packet around each fillet, leaving a little air inside so the ingredients can steam; twist the edges to seal. Place the packets in a shallow baking dish.

Bake until the fish is just cooked through, about 10 to 12 minutes. Remove carefully and serve.

VARIATION Substitute a dry white wine for the sake.

RECOMMENDED WINE
Riesling Clare Valley Polish Hill 2004
Grosset Wines
Auburn, Clare Valley, South Australia

ALTERNATIVES
Riesling or *Gewürztraminer*

GRILLED PRAWNS WRAPPED IN PANCETTA WITH LIME AND CILANTRO

Serves 4

1 pound large prawns (about 16 to 20), tails intact,
    shelled and deveined
½ pound pancetta, thinly sliced
    Sea salt and freshly ground black pepper
    Juice of 2 limes
2 garlic cloves, minced
2 teaspoons fruity extra-virgin olive oil
¼ cup chopped cilantro

Bamboo skewers will be used for grilling. To prepare them, soak 20 bamboo skewers in water for 30 minutes.

Wrap each prawn with one slice of pancetta. With each turn, overlap the pancetta slightly, by about ⅛ inch. It is only necessary to wrap the center of the prawn.

Skewer the prawns, leaving a small space between them on the skewer to allow the heat of the grill to penetrate and cook them. Season to taste with salt and pepper. Refrigerate until ready to grill.

Prepare a lime vinaigrette by whisking together the lime juice, garlic, and olive oil in a small bowl.

Over a hot grill or under a broiler, grill the skewered prawns until they are cooked through. The pancetta will not be completely browned. Do not overcook.

Divide the prawns among 4 plates. Add the cilantro to the lime vinaigrette; drizzle the vinaigrette over the prawns. Serve warm.

NOTES The high acidity of this sauce cuts the richness of the pancetta nicely. The prawns can be wrapped a day in advance and refrigerated; the vinaigrette can also be prepared ahead and refrigerated. The grilling process also works well with radicchio; cooking reduces the bitterness.

VARIATION Substitute prosciutto for the pancetta.

RECOMMENDED WINE
Napa Valley Chardonnay 2004
Peju Province Winery ◆ Rutherford, California

ALTERNATIVES
Chardonnay or *Sauvignon Blanc*

MEDITERRANEAN RED SNAPPER

Serves 4

1 tablespoon extra-virgin olive oil
1 large onion, thinly sliced
3 garlic cloves, crushed
2 cups plum tomatoes, diced, peeled, and seeded
1 jalapeño chili, finely diced and seeded
1 teaspoon crushed red peppers
1 teaspoon cumin
¼ teaspoon ground cinnamon
4 red snapper fillets, 6 ounces each
½ cup sliced green olives

Preheat oven to 350°F.

In a medium skillet, combine the olive oil, onion, and garlic. Cook until the onions are tender, about 10 minutes.

Stir in the tomatoes, jalapeño, red peppers, cumin, and cinnamon. Cook until the mixture is simmering.

Pour the mixture into an 8″ × 12″ baking dish. Put the red snapper and olives on top of the mixture; cover. Bake until the fish flakes easily with a fork, about 25 minutes.

RECOMMENDED WINE
Chardonnay 2002
Seavey Vineyard • St. Helena, California

ALTERNATIVES
Chardonnay or *Pinot Noir*

PAN-SEARED SCALLOPS
IN A CHAMPAGNE GRAPE–WINE SAUCE

Serves 4

16 large sea scallops, side muscles removed
Sea salt and freshly ground pepper to taste
3 tablespoons extra-virgin olive oil
2 tablespoons minced shallots
1 cup halved Champagne grapes
¼ cup white wine
½ cup sliced almonds, toasted
2 tablespoons chopped fresh Italian parsley

Sprinkle the scallops with salt and pepper.

Heat 2 tablespoons of the olive oil in a large nonstick sauté pan over medium-high heat. Add the scallops, and cook 2 minutes per side. Transfer the scallops to warm plate; tent with foil.

Add the remaining 1 tablespoon of olive oil to the same skillet over medium-high heat. Add the shallots and grapes; sauté until the shallots are golden, stirring occasionally, about 2 minutes.

Stir in the wine and any accumulated scallop juices; bring the mixture to boil. Season to taste with salt and pepper. Stir in the almonds and parsley.

Divide the scallops among 4 plates, top with the sauce, and serve.

VARIATION Substitute seedless black grapes for the Champagne grapes.

RECOMMENDED WINE
Dijon Clones Chardonnay 2003
Pine Ridge Winery • Napa, California

ALTERNATIVES
Chardonnay or *Sauvignon Blanc*

GRILLED SALMON
WITH DILL AND GARLIC OVER GREENS

Serves 4

Salmon fillets

- 4 6-ounce salmon fillets
- 2 tablespoons extra-virgin olive oil
- ¼ cup chopped fresh dill
   Sea salt and freshly ground black pepper
- 2 tablespoons crushed garlic

Greens

- 1 to 2 tablespoons olive oil
- 1 to 2 garlic cloves, crushed
- 8 cups organic salad greens
   Sea salt and freshly ground black pepper
- ⅓ cup mild goat cheese
- ¼ cup balsamic vinegar

Prepare the barbecue grill. Remove the salmon from the refrigerator 30 minutes prior to cooking.

To prepare the salmon: Rub both sides of the salmon fillets with olive oil. Sprinkle both sides generously with fresh dill; season to taste with salt and pepper.

Start cooking the salmon flesh side down; sear it quickly on both sides until golden brown. Move it away from direct heat and sprinkle it with crushed garlic to taste. Cook the salmon until it just turns opaque.

To prepare the greens (while the salmon is grilling): Put 1 to 2 tablespoons of olive oil into a large bowl; add the crushed garlic and mash it into the oil with a fork.

Add pre-washed salad greens to the bowl; season to taste with salt and pepper. Add goat cheese and balsamic vinegar, tossing lightly to combine.

Serve the salmon fillets over the greens.

Courtesy of Greg Brown, Calistoga, California

RECOMMENDED WINE
Grenache Napa Valley 2004
T-Vine Cellars ◆ Calistoga, California

ALTERNATIVES
Grenache or *Syrah*

HERB-CRUSTED AHI TUNA

Serves 4

   2 tablespoons whole wheat flour
   ½ teaspoon salt
   ¼ teaspoon freshly ground pepper
   2 tablespoons herbes de Provence
1½ pounds ahi tuna
   1 tablespoon olive oil
   ¼ medium yellow onion, thinly sliced
   2 cups low-salt chicken broth
   1 cup florets from broccoli crown
   1 cup frozen petite peas

In a shallow pan, combine the flour, salt, pepper, and herbes de Provence.

Put each piece of fish into the herb mixture, pressing the fish to thoroughly coat both sides. Set aside.

Heat the oil in a large skillet; add the onion and sauté until the onion softens.

Add the tuna and sauté for 3 minutes on each side. Add the broth, broccoli florets, and frozen peas. Simmer for approximately 10 minutes.

Serve in a shallow soup bowl.

NOTE If herbes de Provence is not available, use chopped parsley, basil, oregano, chives, etc.

VARIATION Substitute halibut for the ahi tuna.

RECOMMENDED WINE
Estate Chardonnay 2002
deLorimier Winery • Geyserville, California

ALTERNATIVES
Chardonnay or *Sauvignon Blanc*

SIXTEEN

DESSERTS

HONEY-GLAZED BAKED APPLES
WITH DRIED FRUIT

Serves 4

4 large tart apples, unpeeled and cored
½ cup mixed dried fruit bits
1 tablespoon minced crystallized ginger
½ teaspoon cinnamon
1 teaspoon grated lemon peel
1 cup unsweetened apple juice or apple cider
4 tablespoons honey

Preheat oven to 350°F.

Cut a thin slice from the bottom of each apple so that the apple will stand upright. Place the apples in a small glass baking dish.

Mix the dried fruit with the ginger, cinnamon, and lemon peel; fill the cored-out section of each apple with 2 tablespoons of the dried fruit mixture. Pour the apple juice around the apples in the dish, and drizzle honey over the dried fruit filling and apples.

Bake the apples until tender when pierced with a skewer, basting frequently with pan juices, about 55 minutes.

Serve warm, spooning pan juices over the apples.

WATERMELON-RASPBERRY SORBET

Serves 4

⅓ cup water
⅓ cup sugar
4 cups diced seedless watermelon pieces (about 3 pounds
    with the rind)
1 cup fresh raspberries
1 cup vanilla yogurt
3 tablespoons fresh lime juice

To prepare a sugar syrup, combine the water and sugar in a small sauce-pan. Cook, stirring over high heat until the sugar is dissolved. Transfer the sugar syrup to a glass measuring cup and let it cool slightly.

Puree the watermelon and raspberries in a food processor or blender, half at a time, pulsing until smooth. Transfer the mixture to a large bowl.

Whisk in the cooled sugar syrup, yogurt, and lime juice until combined. Pour the mixture through a fine-mesh sieve into another large bowl, whisking to release all juice. Discard the pulp.

Pour the extracted juices into an ice-cream maker and freeze according to the manufacturer's directions. (Alternatively, pour into a shallow metal pan and freeze until solid, about 6 hours or overnight. Remove from the freezer to defrost slightly, about 5 minutes. Break the frozen mixture into small chunks and process in a food processor, in batches, until smooth and creamy.)

Serve immediately, or transfer to a storage container and freeze for up to 2 hours.

RED WINE–POACHED PEARS

Serves 4

6 firm Bartlett pears
3 cups hearty red wine, such as Zinfandel
1 cup fresh orange juice
  Zest of 1 orange
2 tablespoons fresh lemon juice
1 cinnamon stick
4 whole cloves
1 bay leaf
1 teaspoon honey
  Plain yogurt, as garnish
  Mint leaves, as garnish

Peel the pears, leaving the stems intact.

In a large saucepan, combine the wine, orange juice and zest, lemon juice, cinnamon, cloves, bay leaf, and honey, and bring to a boil.

Add the pears to the liquid and simmer until tender, about 20 minutes. Cool the pears in the wine mixture to room temperature.

Serve with a spoonful of yogurt and mint leaves as garnish.

STRAWBERRIES IN
BALSAMIC–BLACK PEPPER GLAZE

Serves 4

2 pints strawberries, stemmed
3 tablespoons brown sugar
1 tablespoon freshly ground black pepper
¼ cup balsamic vinegar

Rinse the strawberries in cool water, place in a strainer or colander, and shake off most of the water.

Slice the strawberries about ⅛-inch thick, place them in a large bowl, and sprinkle them with sugar. Cover and refrigerate for at least 1 hour and up to 4 hours.

Preheat the oven to 375°F.

Toss the strawberries with the black pepper; add the balsamic vinegar.

Put the strawberries with all of their juices into a large sauté pan or a large ovenproof dish. Roast until the juices are bubbling and the strawberries are hot but not mushy, about 8 to 10 minutes.

Divide among 4 individual dishes and serve immediately.

Adapted from a recipe by Michele Anna Jordan, Salt & Pepper, *Broadway Books*

ESPRESSO CREAM

Serves 4

1 pound low-fat ricotta cheese
2 tablespoons cocoa powder
1 tablespoon Grand Marnier, or orange-flavored liqueur
  Zest of 1 orange
¼ cup espresso coffee, cold
1 teaspoon vanilla extract
  Dash of ground cinnamon
  Dash of salt
½ cup chestnut honey (or your preference)
  Fresh berries, as garnish

Combine the ricotta cheese, cocoa powder, Grand Marnier, orange zest, espresso, vanilla, cinnamon, and salt in a food processor and puree until smooth. Cover and refrigerate for a few hours.

To serve, spoon the creamy mixture into small glasses, drizzle with honey, and garnish with fresh berries.

GUILT-FREE COOKIES

Makes 2 dozen cookies

¾ cup chopped dried apricots

½ cup dried tart cherries

½ cup chopped dates

1 cup orange juice concentrate

1 tablespoon grated orange zest

1½ cups rolled oats

1 cup whole wheat flour

½ teaspoon salt

1 teaspoon baking soda

½ teaspoon cinnamon

¼ teaspoon nutmeg

1 egg, lightly beaten

½ cup canola oil

½ cup chopped pecans

Preheat oven to 350°F.

In a nonreactive saucepan, combine the apricots, cherries, dates, orange juice concentrate, and orange zest. Simmer over low heat for 15 minutes. Cool.

In a large bowl, combine the oats, flour, salt, baking soda, cinnamon, and nutmeg. Add the egg and oil, mixing until well blended. Stir in the cooled fruit and the pecans.

Line a baking sheet with parchment paper. Drop the batter by teaspoon-fuls onto the baking sheet; flatten each one with a spatula to ¼-inch thickness. Bake for 12 to15 minutes. Cool on a rack.

ORANGE-APRICOT COMPOTE

Serves 4 to 6

1 cup dried apricots
½ cup dried cherries
½ cup golden raisins
2 cups fresh orange juice
2 tablespoons honey
   Plain yogurt, as garnish
   Mint leaves, as garnish

Place the apricots, cherries, raisins, and orange juice in a small bowl and let them stand for 1 hour, until the fruit pieces are plump. Drain, reserving the juice.

Preheat oven to 375°F.

Mix the reserved orange juice with the honey. Put the fruit in a baking dish and cover it with the orange juice mixture. Cover the dish with foil and bake until the juice is nearly absorbed, about 1 hour. Remove from the oven.

Serve either warm or chilled, with yogurt and mint leaves as garnish.

WALNUT-CHOCOLATE-STUFFED FIGS

Serves 6

1 pound dried Calimyrna figs
2 cups port
1½ cups coarsely chopped walnuts
2 teaspoons ground cinnamon
½ teaspoon ground ginger
¼ teaspoon ground cloves
¼ teaspoon nutmeg
2 ounces bittersweet or semisweet chocolate, chopped

In a small saucepan, cover the figs with port and bring them to a simmer. Remove from heat and allow to sit at room temperature for 30 minutes. Drain well.

In a small bowl, combine walnuts, cinnamon, ginger, cloves, and nutmeg.

Preheat oven to 350°F.

Spray a baking dish with nonstick cooking spray.

Make a slash in the bottom of each fig. Fill each fig with the walnut mixture, add a sliver or two of chocolate, and press closed.

Place the figs into the baking dish, cut side down. Cook until heated through and golden, about 20 to 30 minutes.

RECOMMENDED READING

Books

Field, Carol. *The Italian Baker*. New York: HarperCollins, 2000.

Field spent two years working with the bakers of Italy. The result is recipes that are impeccably written for utmost ease and flexibility. Some breads and desserts are simple and earthy, some elegant and refined, but all will be a revelation to Americans who have previously known Italian breads and desserts only from a limited and stereotyped range. Each recipe offers instructions for making dough by hand, by electric mixer, and by food processor. Illustrations provide the step-by-step how-to, and chapters on ingredients, equipment, and technique reveal the whys and wherefores.

Ford, Gene. *The Science of Healthy Drinking*. San Francisco: Wine Appreciation Guild, 2003.

This compilation of scientific information covers the subject of wine and health in broad terms.

Goldstein, Sid. *The Wine Lover's Cookbook: Great Recipes for the Perfect Glass of Wine*. San Francisco: Chronicle Books, 1999.

Goldstein describes in detail the flavor profiles of 13 popular varietals, such as Merlot and Chardonnay, and explains which ingredients balance each wine, giving the reader a professional's foundation for planning meals with each kind of wine. Best of all, he offers 100 recipes, from appetizers to desserts, specifically created to complement a particular varietal.

Kramer, Matt. *New California Wine*. Philadelphia: Running Press, 2004.

This comprehensive exploration of the Napa Valley and California wine production is written by arguably the wittiest, most sincere wine critic of the day.

Kramer, Matt. *A Passion for Piedmont*. New York: Wm. Morrow, 1994.

This combination travel journal, wine guide, and food book explores one of the world's most heralded wine-producing areas: Piedmont, Italy. It is an excellent introduction to the international wine and food scene, simple cooking, and wine people.

Madison, Deborah. *Vegetarian Cooking for Everyone*. New York: Broadway Books, 1997.

The heart of this book is the A to Z vegetable section, with details on vegetables from the common to the exotic, including how to buy them, cook them, and complement them with herbs, sauces, and other partners.

Mondavi, Robert. *Harvests of Joy: My Passion for Excellence*. New York: Harcourt Brace, 1998.

This is the personal story of an iconic figure in the American wine industry. It is a treatise on the history and culture of American wine as told in the autobiography of a truly great wine individual.

Parker, Robert. *Bordeaux: A Consumer's Guide to the World's Finest Wines*. New York: Simon & Schuster, 2003.

This is an authoritative and exhausting review of Bordeaux, the historic quintessential wine-producing region in the southwest of France, written by the wine world's most recognized authority.

Psilakis, Maria and Psilakis, Nikos. *Cretan Cooking, Cretan Diet*. Crete, Greece: Karmanor, 2000.

This book exposes what it has taken the medical community a century to discover—the healthy diet and lifestyle of the island of Crete—with medical references, lifestyle information, and food recipes from Cretan villages.

Sbrocco, Leslie. *Wine for Women: A Guide to Buying, Pairing, and Sharing Wine*. New York: HarperCollins, 2003.

Sbrocco scraps the stuffy winespeak and deals with what women really want to know about wine. The book includes shopping guides with hundreds of recommended wines, quick ideas for wine-friendly meals, and creative tips for sharing wine with family and friends.

Waters, Alice. *Chez Panisse Vegetables*. New York: HarperCollins, 2000.

Waters shares her energy and enthusiasm for what she describes as "living foods." She offers detailed information about the seasonal availability, proper look, flavor, and preparation of each selection.

Werlin, Laura. *The All American Cheese and Wine Book*. New York: Stewart, Tabori & Chang, 2003.

Werlin explains how each cheese is made, what flavor qualities each has, and what types of wines will generally bring out the best in each category of cheese. She offers the same kind of overview for American wines, paying particular attention to those produced by the smaller boutique wineries.

Whitten, David N., and Lipp, Martin R. *To Your Health!: Two Physicians Explore the Health Benefits of Wine*. New York: HarperCollins, 1995.

This is a practical, easy-reading compendium on wine and better health, written by two practicing physicians and wine enthusiasts.

Wolfert, Paula. *Mediterranean Grains and Greens: A Book of Savory, Sun-Drenched Recipes*. New York: HarperCollins, 1998.

Wolfert includes recipes that she considers to be the "great and famous" specialties truly representing the indigenous cooking of a region, but that are undiscovered or unusual.

Articles

Cordain L, Bryan ED, Melby CL, Smith MJ. Influence of moderate daily wine consumption on body weight regulation and metabolism in healthy free-living males. *Journal of the American College of Nutrition* 16:134–139, 1997.

This study shows that adding two glasses of red wine to the evening meal does not adversely affect body weight or promote the development of obesity.

de Lorgeril M, Renaud S, Mamelle N, et al. Mediterranean alpha-linoleic acid-rich diet in secondary prevention of coronary heart disease. *Lancet* 343: 1454–1459, 1994.

Taking a Mediterranean diet to Lyon, France reduced the incidence of heart disease and improved the prognosis of patients who suffered a previous heart attack by greater than 70 percent. This is a landmark study in cardiac prevention.

Goldfinger T. Beyond the French paradox: The impact of moderate beverage alcohol and wine consumption in the prevention of cardiovascular disease. *Cardiology Clinics* 21:449–457, 2003.

This is a comprehensive review of the major world literature supporting the benefits of wine drinking in improved cardiovascular health. It includes an extensive review of epidemiologic data and biological mechanisms, with commentary by the author.

Gronbaek M, Deis A, Sorensen TIA, Becker U, Schnohr P, Jensen G. Mortality associated with moderate intakes of wine, beer, or spirits. *British Medical Journal* 310:1165–1169, 1995.

The authors compare the effects of three alcoholic beverage choices, showing the superior health benefit of wine over beer and spirits.

Renaud S, de Lorgeril M. Wine, alcohol, platelets, and the French paradox for coronary heart disease. *Lancet* 339:1523–1526, 1992.

This insightful report of the cardiac benefits of wine drinking in France revealed a low rate of cardiac disease where the prevailing diet would otherwise have predicted a high incidence of heart disease and cardiac death. The French Paradox presented by Renaud and his colleagues changed the way the world looked at wine drinking and increased red wine consumption by 40 percent in the United States.

Simopoulos, AP. What is so special about the diet of Greece? The scientific evidence. *World Review of Nutrition and Dietetics* 95:80–92, 2005.

This is a comprehensive review of the Mediterranean diet, more specifically the traditional peasant diet of Greece, and the scientific evidence supporting its role in the prevention and treatment of many common diseases of modern society, including coronary heart disease.

Stampfer MJ, Colditz GA, Willett WC, Speizer FE, Hennekens CH. A prospective study of moderate alcohol consumption and risk of coronary disease and stroke in women. *New England Journal of Medicine* 319:267–273, 1988.

The authors report a large-scale observational trial that showed a dramatic benefit to moderate alcohol drinkers, with a greater than 50 percent reduction in major vascular events such as heart attack and stroke.

St Leger AS, Cochrane AL, Moore F. Factors associated with cardiac mortality in developed countries with particular reference to the consumption of wine. *Lancet* 1:1017–1020, 2005.

This seminal epidemiologic study showed the benefits of wine drinking among several of the major world populations. The study predates the report of the French Paradox and provides indisputable evidence that wine drinkers enjoy reduced risk of death from heart disease.

Vadstrup ES, Petersen L, Sorensen TI, Gronbaek M. Waist circumference in relation to history of amount and type of alcohol: results from the Copenhagen City Heart Study. *International Journal of Obesity and Related Metabolic Disorders* 27:238–246, 2003.

This Danish study showed that moderate to high consumption of alcohol and of beer and spirits was associated with later high waist circumference, whereas moderate to high wine consumption may have the opposite effect.

SUBJECT INDEX

diet *see also* Atkins Diet; Crete, diet and
        lifestyle of; low-carbohydrate,
        high-fat diet; low-fat,
        high-carbohydrate diet;
        Mediterranean diet; South Beach
        Diet
    effect of, on cholesterol levels 22, 31
    effect of, on heart disease 31
diseases, effect of moderate wine
        consumption on 26–27
Dolcetto 51, 58, 61, 71, 95, 96

E

endothelium *see also* heart disease
    role of, in protection against heart disease
        17, 25
exercise 2, 8, 17, 88, 92, 103

F

farmers market 86, 87, 96–98
fatty acid(s) 37; *see also* omega-3 fatty
        acid(s)
fish, as source of omega-3 fatty acids 40
flights *see* Wine Lover's Healthy Weight
        Loss Plan
food(s) *see also* diet
    organic 80–81, 86, 102
    pairing with wine 65–78; *see also* wine,
        pairing with food
Framingham project 15–16
French Paradox ix, x, 4–5, 18

G

garlic 92
gewürztraminer 58, 60, 68, 70, 72, 87
Glycemic Index (GI) 42
grape juice, purple, vs. red wine, in effect
        on health 24–25
greens *see* Mediterranean diet
grenache 51, 62

H

health risks 43
heart attack
    incidence of 17
    risk of, and obesity viii, 2
heart disease *see also* endothelium; wine,
        moderate consumption of,
        benefits of
    cost of managing 28

defined 16–17
effect of fatty acids on 37–39
Framingham project study of 15–16
incidence 3, 16
prevention of, in childhood, 43
risk factors
    high blood pressure 4
    high serum cholesterol levels 4, 24–26
    smoking 4
role of diet in 31, 33
and weight loss vii
high blood pressure
    as modifiable health risk 43
    and obesity viii
    as risk factor in heart disease 4, 15–16,
        17
high-density lipoprotein (HDL)
        see cholesterol
high fructose corn syrup 101
hypertension *see* high blood pressure

J

J-shaped curve 19–21

L

Lipid Research Clinics Coronary Primary
        Prevention Trial 32
low-carbohydrate, high-fat diet, and weight
        loss vii, 3
low-density lipoprotein (LDL)
        see cholesterol
low-fat, high-carbohydrate diet
    effect of, on heart disease viii, 32–33,
        100
    effect of, on obesity 33
    effect of, on type 2 diabetes 33
    and weight loss vii–viii, 3, 100
Lyon Diet Heart Study 5, 39

M

medications, taken while drinking wine 29
Mediterranean diet v, ix, 92; *see also* Crete,
        diet and lifestyle of
    adherence to 45–46
    benefits of 36–41, 44–46, 100
    composition of 6, 82–84
    Lyon Diet Heart Study of 5
merlot 1, 49, 58, 61, 62, 66, 68, 72, 75
metabolism 33–34
microclimate 50

moderation *see* wine, moderate
consumption of; Wine Lover's
Healthy Weight Loss Plan,
components of
monounsaturated fats 41, 82; *see also* fatty
acid(s); omega-3 fatty acid(s)
mortality, obesity and risk of viii

N
Nebbiolo grape 50, 61, 66

O
obesity *see also* overweight
defined by Body Mass Index 98
effect of, on diseases and medical
conditions 33
effect of poor diet and lifestyle on viii, 33
incidence viii
as modifiable health risk 43
olive oil, as major source of fat in
Mediterranean diet 36–37
omega-3 fatty acid(s) *see also* alpha-linoleic
acid; fatty acid(s)
compared to omega-6 fatty acids 38
effect of, on diseases and medical
conditions 37–40, 41
sources of 38, 72, 82
in The Wine Lover's Healthy Weight Loss
Plan 6
omega-6 fatty acid(s) *see* omega-3 fatty
acid(s)
organic food(s) *see* food(s), organic
overweight *see also* obesity
defined by Body Mass Index 98
incidence viii, 2

P
parsley, Italian 83
physical activity *see* exercise
Pinot Blanc 60, 70, 71
Pinot Gris/Pinot Grigio 60, 66, 71, 75
Pinot Noir 1, 55, 56, 58, 61, 62, 66, 75, 87, 88
polyphenols *see* wine, components of
polyunsaturated fats 41, 82; *see also* fatty
acid(s)

R
red grapes, list of 60
red wine(s) 60–62
aging 56–57

bottling 59
pairing with food 62; *see also* wine,
pairing with food
Renaud, Serge Charles v, x, 4, 15, 23, 26, 35,
36
resveratrol 25–26
Riesling 48, 58, 60, 68, 70, 71, 75, 87
rosé 51, 62

S
sauvignon blanc 1, 58, 59–60, 69, 71, 87
Seven Countries Study 44
shiraz 61, 67, 69, 75, 88
Slow Food Association/Slow Food
Movement 99
smell of wine 76
smoking
as modifiable health risk 43
as risk factor in heart disease 4, 15–16, 17
South Beach Diet x
sparkling wine(s) 54
sugar, white 101
syrah *see* shiraz

T
tasting wine *see* wine, tasting
trans fat(s) 100

V
varietal wine(s), defined 49
vineyard(s) 50, 51–54;
see also microclimate
organic vs. chemical protection of, against
predators and disease 53
water as a resource 54
viticulture 53; *see also* vineyard(s)

W
water
for drinking 103
as a resource for vineyards 54
weight, and wine consumption 2
weight loss
benefits of vii
through diet 80
white grapes, list of 60
white sugar 101
white wine(s) 59–60
aging 56–57
bottling 59

RECIPE INDEX

cheese (*continued*)
Romaine Hearts with Gorgonzola-Walnut
 Vinaigrette 165
Saturday Night Pizza with Caramelized
 Onions, Leeks, and Gorgonzola 142
Tomato, Watermelon, and Feta Salad 152
Tortellini, Spinach, and Tomato Soup 184
Chicken Breasts Stuffed with Artichokes
 and Goat Cheese 234
Chicken Breasts with Fresh Mozzarella 238
Chicken Coleslaw, Asian 159
Chicken Diablo Soup 180
Chicken Dukkah Salad 158
Chicken Lettuce Wraps, Asian 232
Chicken Poached in Orange Juice and Fresh
 Rosemary 239
Chicken Salad, Strawberry 172
Chicken Salad, Warm Asian 166
Chicken with Mint Sauce, Moroccan Grilled
 236
Chicken with Wild Greens Salad,
 Parmesan-Crusted 230
Chickpea Artichoke Salad 167
Clams Oreganta 138
Coleslaw, Asian Chicken 159
Cookies, Guilt-Free 273
Corn, Papaya, and Black Bean Salad with
 Toasted Cumin Seed Dressing, Grilled
 170
Corn Polenta, Fresh 197
Corn Waffles, Savory 114
Couscous, Lemon-Mint 207
Crab, Asian Watermelon-Cucumber Soup
 with 188
Crab, Mango, and Ginger Salad 171
Crostini with Gorgonzola, Caramelized
 Onions, and Pine Nuts 124
Cucumber Yogurt Dressing, Wild Greens
 and Shrimp with 164
Cucumbers Stuffed with Feta and Herbs 126

D

Dijon Balsamic Vinaigrette 174
Duck Breast with Mushroom Sauce, Sautéed
 244

E

Eggplant Dip, Spicy Asian 134
Eggplant with Tahini, Roasted (Baba
 Ghanoush) 128

Eggs Provençale 108
eggs
Avocado, Shrimp, and Manchego Cheese
 Omelet 119
Breakfast Bruschetta 110
Breakfast Frittata 115
Eggs Provençale 108
Smoked Salmon Hash 117
Espresso Cream 272

F

Fajitas, Beef 212
Fig and Walnut Tapenade 141
Figs, Walnut-Chocolate–Stuffed 275
Fish en Papillote, Asian 258
Fish Stew, Mediterranean 252
Frittata, Breakfast 115
fruits
Apple, Walnut, and Pomegranate Salad
 153
Apple-Onion Omelet 116
Asian Watermelon-Cucumber Soup
 with Crab 188
Beet, Orange, and Mint Salad 148
Breakfast Polenta with Dried Fruit
 and Hazelnuts 118
Chicken Poached in Orange Juice and
 Fresh Rosemary 239
Chunky Ginger Five-Spice Applesauce
 113
Crab, Mango, and Ginger Salad 171
Fig and Walnut Tapenade 141
Gingered Butternut Squash and Apple
 Soup 185
Grilled Corn, Papaya, and Black Bean
 Salad with Toasted Cumin Seed
 Dressing 170
Guilt-Free Cookies 273
Honey-Glazed Baked Apples with Dried
 Fruit 268
Irish Oatmeal with Walnuts and Figs 109
Oatmeal Raisin Pancakes 112
Orange-Apricot Compote 274
Orange-Chipotle Scallops 247
Pan-Roasted Orange Carrots 192
Pan-Seared Scallops in a Champagne
 Grape–Wine Sauce 263
Red Wine–Poached Pears 270
Strawberries in Balsamic–Black Pepper
 Glaze 271

About the Authors

Dr. Tedd M. Goldfinger is a board-certified cardiologist and a Fellow of the American College of Cardiology and the American College of Chest Physicians, as well as a member of the American College of Physicians. He is a Clinical Assistant Professor at the University of Arizona College of Medicine.

Dr. Goldfinger is senior cardiologist and president of Desert Cardiology of Tucson Heart Center and founder of the Desert Heart Foundation. He is director of the Wine & Heart Health Research Initiative, an international collaborative group of research scientists on wine and cardiovascular disease prevention.

In addition to his duties as a cardiologist, he is a professional member of the American Society of Enology and Viticulture. He is also involved in a vineyard venture in Cochise County, Arizona, near his home in Tucson.

Dr. Goldfinger is widely published and is a frequent speaker to medical and community organizations on the health benefits of wine and wine appreciation.

The Goldfinger family has recently acquired a home in the Langhe hills of Piedmont, in northern Italy, adjacent to hearty vineyards of Dolcetto and Barbera grapes.

Lynn F. Nicholson brings more than 30 years of travel and culinary expertise to this book. She is a coauthor of *Healthy Spa Cuisine: 400 Signature Recipes from the World's Top Spas.*

Ms. Nicholson graduated with highest honors from the Le Cordon Bleu Culinary Arts Program at the Western Culinary Institute. She has worked for a winery in Oregon's Willamette Valley, and she has run a small catering company. It is through this experience that she gained her expertise, her imaginative recommendations, and her commonsense approach to the topic.

Ms. Nicholson knows firsthand what it means to diet. When she was a teenager at boarding school, she gained more than 50 pounds, weighing 165 at the age of 18! She has tried every diet that exists, and only The Wine Lover's Healthy Weight Loss Plan worked—and continues to work—for her.

When she is not cooking and writing, she breeds Arabian horses on her ranch in central Oregon.